THE ESSENTIAL SWEET POTATO COOKBOOK

100 Delicious Recipes to Enjoy the Nutritious and Versatile Sweet Potato

Ruth Davis

Copyright Material ©2023

All Rights Reserved

No part of this book may be used or transmitted in any form or by any means without the proper written consent of the publisher and copyright owner, except for brief quotations used in a review. This book should not be considered a substitute for medical, legal, or other professional advice.

TABLE OF CONTENTS

TABLE OF CONTENTS 3
INTRODUCTION 7
BREAKFAST 8
   1. Spicy South-western Breakfast Bowl 9
   2. Chocolate Waffle Sundae 11
   3. Breakfast Skillet 14
   4. Sweet potato hash egg skillet 16
   5. Eggs in Nests 18
   6. Barbecue Hash 20
   7. Sweet Potato Pecan Bourbon Waffles 22
   8. Waffled Sweet Potato Gnocchi 25
   9. Sweet potato toasts 28
   10. Breakfast Sweet Potato with Hibiscus Tea Yogurt 30
   11. Sausage-Sweet Potato Hash and Eggs 33
   12. Sweet Potato and Egg Skillet 35
   13. Fried sweet potato hashbrowns 37
   14. Goat cheese, sweet potato & crouton omelets 39

APPETIZERS 42
   15. Sweet Potatoes & Apples in Rum 43
   16. Stuffed Sweet Potatoes 45
   17. Stuffed Sweet Potato on Arugula 47
   18. Chiles Anchos Rellenos 49
   19. Sweet Potato and Carrot Tinga Tacos 52
   20. ROASTED ROOTS PIZZA 54
   21. Sweet potato latkes 57
   22. Daigaku imo 59
   23. Quinoa muffin bites 61
   24. Turmeric Sweet Potato Patties 63
   25. Sweet potato nachos 66

26. Sweet potato Marshmallow bites 68
27. Ceviche Peruano 70
28. Gingered sweet-potato fritters 72

BURGERS, WRAPS, AND SANDWICHES 74

29. Quinoa and Sweet Potato Burger 75
30. Lentil rice burgers 78
31. Spicy Sweet Potato & Black Bean Taquitos 80

MAIN COURSE 83

32. Spicy Chicken Quarters With Sweet Potatoes 84
33. Garlic Florentine Sweet Potatoes 87
34. Risotto with Green Beans and Sweet Potatoes 89
35. Baked Salmon and Sweet Potatoes 91
36. Salmon Teriyaki with Vegetables 94
37. Salmon with sweet potatoes and beans 97
38. Matcha Steamed Cod 99
39. Sweet Potato Marshmallow Casserole 101
40. Cold roast duck with vegetables 103
41. Buffalo Tempeh Harvest Bowls 105

SOUPS AND CURRIES 108

42. Crockpot chicken soup 109
43. Thai Coconut-Curry Flounder 111
44. Crockpot Carrot ginger soup 113
45. Bouillon Soup 115
46. Curried Lentils with Sweet Potatoes and Chickpeas 118
47. Mexican Beef And Sweet Potato Broth Soup 120
48. Sweet potato and Tequila soup 123
49. Red Bean Stew from Jamaica 125
50. Chicken Soup 127
51. Corn Soup 130

52. Salmon Vegetable Chowder 133

53. Ground bison and vegetable stew 135

54. Coconut Beef Curry 137

55. Sweet potato and pumpkin soup 139

56. Thai Sweet Potato Curry 142

57. Thai Curry Hot Pot 144

58. Spicy Sweet Potato Kale Cannellini Soup 147

59. Sweet Potato Chicken Stew 150

60. Sweet Potato Lentil Stew 152

61. Callaloo Soup 154

62. Chickpea Sweet Potato Stew 157

63. Coconut Curry Lentils 159

PASTA 161

64. Chestnut and Sweet potato Gnocchi 162

65. Bucatini with Pesto and Sweet Potatoes 166

66. Chestnut and Sweet potato Gnocchi 169

SIDES 173

67. Lime and tequila sweet potatoes 174

68. Sweet Potato Bacon Mash 176

69. Stir-Fried Sweet Potatoes with Parmesan 178

70. Sweet Potatoes with Tamarind 180

71. Fall vegetables on the grill 182

72. Chimichurri grilled vegetables 184

73. Roasted-Garlic Sweet Potatoes 186

74. Sous Vide Maple Glazed Sweet Potatoes 188

75. Bacon & Sweet Potatoes 190

76. Gouda Mixed Potato Mash 192

77. Two-Tone Baked Sweet Potatoes 194

78. Chili sweet potato gratin 196

SALADS 198

79. Arugula and Sweet Potato Salad 199
80. Autumn Harvest Salad 201
81. Sweet Potato And Broccoli With Pomegranate Dressing 203
82. Collard Green Salad with Sweet Potatoes 205
83. Sweet Potato Salad with almonds 207
84. Quinoa Mango Salad With Mashed Potatoes 209
85. Grilled Three-Potato Salad 211
86. Roasted Sweet Potato and Prosciutto Salad 213
87. Roasted Vegetable and Polenta Salad 215
88. Roasted Sweet Potatoes & Fresh Figs 218
89. Caesar Salad with BBQ Sweet Potato Croutons 220
90. Sweet Potato & Avocado Green Salad 223

DESSERT 225

91. Chicken Pie with Sweet Potatoes 226
92. Coconut sweet potato pudding 228
93. Sweet Potato Pie Trifle 230
94. Sweet Potato Pie Tiramisu 232
95. Cherry-sweet potato bread 235
96. Cranberry sweet potato muffins 237
97. Grated sweet potato pudding 239

DRINKS 241

98. Apple Pie Juice 242
99. Sweet Potato Pie Protein Shake 244
100. Sweet Potato Shake 246

CONCLUSION 248

INTRODUCTION

Sweet potatoes are a versatile and nutritious root vegetable that can be used in a variety of dishes, from sweet to savory. This cookbook celebrates the sweet potato with 100 delicious recipes that will delight your taste buds and nourish your body.

Whether you prefer sweet or savory dishes, this cookbook has something for everyone. From sweet potato pancakes and muffins to soups, stews, and curries, this cookbook will inspire you to explore the many ways you can incorporate sweet potatoes into your meals.

Each recipe is accompanied by a colorful image that will make your mouth water and inspire you to try out new dishes. The recipes are easy to follow, with step-by-step instructions that will guide you through the cooking process.

In addition to being delicious, sweet potatoes are also packed with nutrients. They are an excellent source of fiber, vitamins, and minerals, including vitamin A, vitamin C, and potassium. With this cookbook, you can enjoy the health benefits of sweet potatoes while indulging in delicious meals..

BREAKFAST

1. Spicy South-western Breakfast Bowl

Makes: 2

INGREDIENTS
- 2 sweet potatoes, peeled and diced
- Extra virgin olive oil, for drizzling
- Pinch Salt and pepper
- 1 teaspoon chili powder
- 2 strips of chicken bacon
- ½ medium yellow onion, diced
- ½ green bell pepper, diced
- ½ red bell pepper, diced
- 1 jalapeño, seeded and diced
- 2-3 cups fresh spinach
- 2 eggs
- 1 teaspoon ghee
- 1 avocado, pitted and diced

INSTRUCTIONS:
a) Preheat the oven to 375 degrees F.
b) Place the sweet potatoes on a baking sheet and toss with a drizzle of olive oil.
c) Season with salt, pepper, and chili powder.
d) Bake for 20 minutes, turning once.
e) Cook the chicken bacon in a skillet; set aside.
f) Add the peppers, onion, and jalapeño to the skillet; sauté for 6 minutes.
g) Add in the spinach and cook well.
h) In another skillet, melt the ghee.
i) Cook the eggs, seasoning with salt and pepper.
j) Serve the sweet potatoes and top with the veggie mixture, followed by the egg, crumbled chicken bacon, and avocado.

2. Chocolate Waffle Sundae

Makes 4 SERVINGS

INGREDIENTS
- 1 Cup Cooked Sweet Potatoes (About 1 Large Sweet Potato)
- 1½ Cups All-Purpose Flour
- 2 Tablespoons Brown Sugar
- 1 ½ Teaspoon Baking Powder
- ½ Teaspoon Kosher Salt
- ¼ Teaspoon Baking Soda
- 1 Cup Buttermilk
- 2 Large Eggs
- ½ Cup Pecans
- 2 Tablespoons Unsalted Butter, Melted
- 1 Tablespoons Light Brown Sugar
- Bourbon Syrup:
- 1 Cup Pure Maple Syrup
- 2 Tablespoons Unsalted Butter2 Tablespoons Bourbon

Directions

a) In a medium bowl combine the flour, sugar, cocoa powder, baking powder and salt. In a small saucepan over medium heat melt the butter and chocolate together and set aside to cool slightly.

b) Whisk in the melted butter and chocolate into the flour, plus the milk, vanilla extract and egg yolks.

c) In a clean, medium bowl whisk the egg whites vigorously until they reach soft peaks. Scoop out 1/3 of the whisked egg whites and gently fold it into the waffle batter, careful not to deflate the egg whites.

d) Continue with the remaining white 1/3 at a time.

e) Turn on the waffle iron and preheat until the flame icon stops flashing. Then brush with melted butter or spray with baking spray.

f) Pour in about ½ cup of batter into the center of the waffle iron and close the top.

g) Flip the waffle iron 180° after you close the top and cook for about 2 minutes.

h) After about two minutes you should have a nice golden color. If you want it done a little more, close the top and press the "a bit more" button.

i) Transfer to a rimmed baking sheet with a cooling rack placed on top.

j) Keep the waffles in a 250° oven to stay warm.

k) Repeat with the remaining batter. To serve: Place 2-3 scoops of ice cream on top of a waffle and top with chocolate sauce, caramel sauce and whipped cream.

3. Breakfast Skillet

Makess: 2

INGREDIENTS:
- 1 large or 2 small sweet potatoes peeled and cut into cubes
- 1/2 cup green pepper diced
- 1/2 cup onion diced
- 1/2 cup mushroom diced
- 1 roma tomato diced
- 2 tablespoons cheddar cheese shredded
- 2 eggs
- 2 teaspoons Coconut oil
- 2 teaspoons cumin
- Fresh ground black pepper to taste

Directions
a) On a baking pan, drizzle oil over sweet potato cubes, season with cumin and black pepper and mix well.
b) Bake for 30 minutes, until browned and crispy.
c) When potatoes are about halfway through baking, heat olive oil in a skillet over medium-high heat.
d) Sauté the green pepper, onion, and mushrooms.
e) When potatoes are done, mix well with veggies.
f) Remove from heat, add tomato, and set aside. Sprinkle with cheese.

4. Sweet potato hash egg skillet

Servings: 1

Ingredients
- 1 pound of sweet potatoes, cubed
- 1/4 yellow onion, diced
- 1 large garlic clove, minced
- 1 tablespoon extra-virgin olive oil
- 1/2 teaspoon ground coriander
- 1/4 teaspoon salt
- 2 large eggs
- 1 teaspoon smoked paprika

Toppings
- Broccoli Microgreens
- Toasted Pepitas
- Red pepper flakes

Directions

a) In a medium-low skillet, heat an 8" or 10" skillet.
b) Add the onions and garlic should be added after the olive oil.
c) Cook for 4–5 minutes, or until the onion is translucent and fragrant.
d) Add the sweet potatoes and simmer, turning regularly, for 12 to 15 minutes, or until golden and soft.
e) Simmer for another minute after adding the spices and salt.
f) Make two wells in the sweet potatoes. Add the eggs and cook until the egg whites are set and the yolks have reached your desired consistency, around 10 to 12 minutes.
g) Garnish the egg skillet with microgreens, toasted pepitas, and red pepper flakes before serving.

5. Eggs in Nests

Makes: 6 servings

INGREDIENTS:
- 1 pound sweet potatoes, peeled
- 2 tablespoons olive oil
- 1/4 teaspoon salt, divided
- 1/4 teaspoon black pepper, divided
- 12 large eggs

INSTRUCTIONS:
a) Preheat the oven to 400 degrees Fahrenheit.
b) Using cooking spray, coat a 12-cup muffin tray.
c) Using a box grater, shred potatoes and set aside. In a large skillet, heat the olive oil over medium-high heat. 1/8 teaspoon salt, 1/8 teaspoon pepper, diced sweet potatoes
d) Cook potatoes until soft, about 5-6 minutes. Remove from heat and set aside until cool enough to handle.
e) In each muffin cup, press 1/4 cup cooked potatoes. In the bottom and sides of the muffin cup, press firmly.
f) Coat the potatoes with cooking spray and bake for 5-10 minutes, or until the sides are gently browned.
g) In each sweet potato nest, crack an egg and season with the remaining 1/8 teaspoon salt and 1/8 teaspoon pepper.
h) Bake for 15-18 minutes, or until egg whites and yolks are cooked to desired doneness.
i) Set aside for 5 minutes to cool before removing from pan. Serve and have fun!

6. Barbecue Hash

Ingredient

- 3 sweet potatoes, peeled and chopped
- 1 (8-ounce) package tempeh, chopped
- 1 onion, finely chopped
- 1 red bell pepper, finely chopped
- 1 tablespoon store-bought barbecue sauce
- 1 teaspoon Cajun seasoning
- ¼ cup chopped fresh parsley
- 4 eggs Hot-pepper sauce (optional)

Directions

a) Heat 3 tablespoons of the oil in a large nonstick skillet over medium-high heat. Add the sweet potatoes and tempeh and cook, stirring occasionally, for 5 minutes, or until the mixture begins to brown. Reduce the heat to medium.

b) Add the onion and bell pepper and cook for 12 minutes longer, stirring more frequently at the end of the cooking time, until the tempeh is browned and the potatoes are tender.

c) Add the barbecue sauce, Cajun seasoning, and parsley. Toss to combine, then divide among 4 serving plates.

d) Wipe out the skillet with a paper towel. Reduce the heat to medium-low and add the remaining 1 tablespoon oil. Break the eggs into the skillet and cook to the desired doneness.

e) Slide an egg on top of each portion of the hash and serve at once. Pass hot-pepper sauce, if desired, at the table.

7. Sweet Potato Pecan Bourbon Waffles

Makes 4 SERVINGS

INGREDIENTS

- 2 ½ -3LBS pork shoulder fo he rub
- 2 teaspoons chili powder
- 2 teaspoons cumin powder
- 2 teaspoons kosher salt
- 1 teaspoon paprika
- 1 teaspoon black pepper
- ½ teaspoon garlic powder
- ½ teaspoon onion powder
- ½ TEASPOON Cayenne pepper

FOR THE BARBECUE SAUCE:

- 1 large onion, chopped
- 3 garlic cloves, minced
- 1 ½ cups ketchup
- ½ cup brown sugar
- 2 tablespoons apple cide vinegar
- 4 teaspoons worcestershire   sauce
- 1 teaspoon cayenne pepper
- 1 teaspoon kosher salt
- 1 tablespoons bourbon

Fo he waffles

- 1 ½ cups all-purpose flour
- ¾ cups yellow cornmeal
- 1 tablespoons cane sugar
- 2 teaspoons baking powder
- 1 teaspoon baking soda
- ½ teaspoon kosher salt
- 1½ cups buttermilk
- 2 large eggs
- 2 tablespoons unsalted butter,melted
- ¼ cup honey

DIRECTIONS

a) In a medium bowl, mash the sweet potato with the back of a fork and then combine the flour, brown sugar, baking powder, salt and baking soda. Whisk in the buttermilk, eggs and melted butter.

b) Stir in the melted butter until no dry spots remain. Turn on the waffle iron and preheat until the flame icon stops flashing. Then brush with melted butter or spray with baking spray.

c) Pour in about ½ cup of batter into the center of the waffle iron and close the top. Flip the waffle iron 180° after you close the top and cook for about 2 minutes. After about two minutes you should have a nice golden color. If you want it done a little more, close the top and press the "a bit more" button.

d) Transfer to a rimmed baking sheet with a cooling rack placed on top. Keep the waffles in a 250° oven to stay warm.

e) Repeat with the remaining batter. While the waffles are cooking, in a medium saucepan over medium heat combine the syrup, butter, bourbon and brown sugar and bring to a simmer. Cook for about 2 minutes.

f) Serve the waffles with the warm syrup on top.

g) Leftover waffles can be frozen for up to 3 months. Pour extra syrup in a bottle and store the refrigerator for up to 1 month.

h) Warm before serving.

8. Waffled Sweet Potato Gnocchi

Makes: Serves 4 (makes about 60 gnocchi)

INGREDIENTS
- 1 large baking potato (such as russet) and 1 large sweet potato (about 1½ pounds total)
- 1¼ cups all-purpose flour, plus more for flouring the work surface
- ½ cup grated Parmesan cheese
- 1 teaspoon salt
- ½ teaspoon freshly ground black pepper
- Dash of grated nutmeg (optional)
- 1 large egg, beaten
- Nonstick cooking spray or melted butter
- Pesto or Waffled Sage and Butter Sauce

INSTRUCTIONS:
a) Preheat the oven to 350°F.
b) Bake the potatoes until easily pierced with a fork, about an hour. Let the potatoes cool slightly, then peel them.
c) Pass the potatoes through a food mill or a ricer or grate them over the large holes of a box grater and into a large bowl.
d) Add the 1¼ cups flour to the potatoes and use your hands to mix them together, breaking up any lumps of potato along the way. Sprinkle the cheese, salt, pepper, and nutmeg over the dough and knead lightly to distribute evenly.
e) Once the flour and potatoes are combined, make a well in the center of the bowl and add the beaten egg. Using your fingers, work the egg through the dough until it starts to come together. It will be slightly sticky.
f) On a lightly floured surface, gently knead the dough a few times to bring it together. It should be moist, but not wet and sticky. If it's too sticky, add 1 tablespoon flour at a time, up to ¼ cup. Roll the dough into a log and cut it into 4 pieces.

g) Roll each piece into a rope about the diameter of your thumb and then use a sharp knife to cut into 1-inch segments.

h) Preheat the waffle iron on medium. Coat both sides of the waffle iron grid with nonstick spray, or butter the grids using a silicone pastry brush.

i) Turn down the oven to its lowest setting and set aside a baking sheet to keep the finished gnocchi warm.

j) Gently shake off any residual flour from the gnocchi and place a batch on the waffle iron, leaving a bit of space for each to expand. Close the lid and cook until the grid marks on the gnocchi are golden brown, 2 minutes.

k) Repeat with the remaining gnocchi, keeping the cooked gnocchi warm on the baking sheet in the oven.

l) Serve hot with Pesto Sauce or Waffled Sage and Butter Sauce.

9. Sweet potato toasts

INGREDIENTS:
- 2 large sweet potatoes, sliced into.
- ¼-inch-thick slices.
- 1 tablespoon avocado oil.
- 1 teaspoons salt ½ cup guacamole.
- ½ cup tomatoes, sliced.

INSTRUCTIONS:
a) Preheat your oven to 425° F.
b) Cover a baking sheet with parchment paper.
c) Rub the potato slices with oil and salt and place them on a baking sheet. Bake for 5 minutes in the oven, then flip and bake again for 5 minutes.
d) Top the baked slices with guacamole and tomatoes.

10. Breakfast Sweet Potato with Hibiscus Tea Yogurt

Makes: 2

INGREDIENTS
- 2 purple sweet potato

FOR THE GRANOLA:
- 2 ½ cups oats
- 2 teaspoons dried turmeric
- 1 teaspoon cinnamon
- 1 Tablespoon citrus zest
- ¼ cup honey
- ¼ cup sunflower oil
- ½ cup pumpkin seeds
- dash of salt

FOR THE YOGURT:
- 1 cup plain Greek yogurt
- 1 teaspoon maple syrup
- 1 hibiscus tea bag
- edible flowers, for garnish

INSTRUCTIONS
a) Preheat oven to 425 degrees and poke the potatoes all over with a fork.

b) Wrap the potatoes in tin foil and bake for 45 minutes to one hour.

c) Remove from oven and let cool.

FOR THE GRANOLA:

d) Lower oven heat to 250 degrees and line a baking sheet with parchment paper.

e) Combine all of the granola ingredients in a mixing bowl and stir until everything is coated with the honey and oil.

f) Transfer to the lined baking sheet and spread out as evenly as possible.

g) Bake for 45 minutes, stirring every 15 minutes, or until the granola has browned.

h) Remove from oven and let cool.

FOR THE YOGURT:

i) Make hibiscus tea according to the tea bag's directions and set it aside to cool.

j) Once at room temperature, whisk the maple syrup and tea into the yogurt until you reach a smooth and creamy texture with a slightly pink hue to it.

TO ASSEMBLE:

k) Slice the potatoes in half and top with granola, flavored yogurt, and edible flowers for garnish.

11. Sausage-Sweet Potato Hash and Eggs

Makes: 4

INGREDIENTS:
- Eggs, large 4
- Salt 1/4 teaspoon
- Pecans (chopped) 1/4 cup
- Green onions (sliced) 4
- Cranberries (dried) 1/4 cup
- Granny smith apples, medium (chopped) 2
- Sweet potatoes, cubed (peeled and 1/4-inch cubes each) 2 Italian turkey sausage links (without casings) 4 1/8 cups

INSTRUCTIONS:
a) Take a large-sized skillet that is coated using the cooking spray, cook the sweet potatoes and the sausages over medium flame for 8 to 10 minutes until the sausage is not pink anymore, breaking the sausage into crumbles.
b) Add salt, pecans, cranberries, and apple, cook and mix for 4 to 6 minutes until the potatoes are tender.
c) Remove the mixture from the pan, sprinkle some green onions. Keep it warm.
d) Wipe the skillet clean and use the cooking spray to coat it again; place the skillet over medium-high flame.
e) Break the eggs into the pan one after the other. Lower the flame to low. Cook until the desired doneness is achieved. Turn after the whites are set if you prefer.
f) Serve it with the hash.

12. Sweet Potato and Egg Skillet

Makes: 4

INGREDIENTS:
- Pepper (coarsely ground) 1/8 teaspoon
- Eggs, large 4
- Baby spinach (fresh) 2 cups
- Dried thyme 1/8 teaspoon
- Salt (divided) 1/2 teaspoon
- Garlic clove (minced) 1
- Sweet potatoes, medium (shredded and cubed) 4 cups
- Butter 2 tablespoons

INSTRUCTIONS:
a) Take a heavy skillet or a large cast-iron.
b) Heat the butter in it over a low flame.
c) Add thyme, 1/4 teaspoon of salt, garlic, and sweet potatoes.
d) Cover it and cook for 4 to 5 minutes until the potatoes turn tender. Stir periodically.
e) Mix the spinach in it and stir for 2 to 3 minutes until it wilts.
f) Use the back of a spoon to make four wells in the mixture of potatoes.
g) Break one of the eggs into each of the wells.
h) Sprinkle some pepper and the salt that is remaining on the eggs. Cover it and cook for 5 to 7 minutes on medium-low flame until the egg whites are set entirely, and the yolk begins to thicken but make sure it is not hard.

13. Fried sweet potato hashbrowns

Makes: 8 servings

INGREDIENTS:
- ½ pounds diced bacon
- 1 cup chopped onions
- 1 salt; to taste
- 1 freshly-ground black pepper; to taste
- 1 tablespoon chopped garlic
- 2 pounds sweet potatoes; peeled, grated

INSTRUCTIONS:

a) In a large skillet, render the bacon until crispy, about 8 minutes.

b) Add the onions. Season with salt and pepper.

c) Saute the onions until soft, about 2 minutes.

d) Add the garlic and sweet potatoes. Season with salt and pepper.

e) Saute for about 10 to 15 minutes. Remove from the heat and serve warm.

14. Goat cheese, sweet potato & crouton omelets

Makes: 2 Servings

INGREDIENTS:
- 2 tablespoon Unsalted butter
- 1 cup Half-inch cubes country-style bread
- 1 medium Sweet potato -; (abt 1/2 lb)
- 1 small Red onion; sliced thin
- 2 ounce Soft mild goat cheese; crumbled
- 1 teaspoon Minced fresh rosemary leaves
- 5 large Eggs
- Salt; to taste
- Freshly-ground black pepper; to taste

INSTRUCTIONS:

a) Preheat oven to 350 degrees. In an 8-inch non-stick skillet, melt 1 tablespoon butter over moderate heat and in a bowl toss with bread cubes.

b) On a baking sheet toast bread cubes in middle of oven until pale golden and crisp, about 10 minutes, and transfer to a bowl.

c) Peel sweet potato and cut into ¼-inch dice. In a steamer set over boiling water steam potato and onion until tender, about 4 minutes, and toss with croutons. Cool mixture and toss with goat cheese and rosemary. In a bowl whisk together eggs and salt and pepper to taste.

d) In skillet heat ½ tablespoon butter over moderately-high heat until foam subsides. Pour in half of eggs, tilting skillet to spread evenly over bottom.

e) Cook omelet 1 minute, or until almost set, stirring top layer with back of a fork and shaking skillet, letting any uncooked egg run underneath.

f) Sprinkle half of omelet with half of crouton mixture and cook 1 minute more, or until set. Fold omelet over filling and transfer to a plate.

g) Keep omelet warm while making another omelet with remaining butter, eggs and crouton mixture in same manner.

APPETIZERS

15. Sweet Potatoes & Apples in Rum

Makes: 6

INGREDIENTS:
- ¼ teaspoon black pepper
- 3 sweet potatoes, scrubbed and pricked with a fork
- ½ teaspoon ground cinnamon
- 1 tablespoon apple cider vinegar
- ½ teaspoon kosher salt
- 2 tablespoons dark rum
- 1 tablespoon unsalted butter

TOPPING
- 2 cups peeled and chopped Granny Smith apples
- Fresh sage leaves
- 3 tablespoons chopped pecans, toasted

INSTRUCTIONS:
a) Combine all the ingredients, except the topping, in a 6-quart Crockpot.

b) Slow cook until the potatoes are tender, about 6 hours.

c) Remove the potatoes, and cut them in half lengthwise.

d) Top with apples, pecans, and sage leaves.

16. **Stuffed Sweet Potatoes**

Makes: 1

INGREDIENTS:
- 1 cup water
- 1 sweet potato
- 1 tablespoon pure maple syrup
- 1 tablespoon almond butter
- 1 tablespoon chopped pecans
- 2 tablespoons blueberries
- 1 teaspoon chia seeds
- 1 teaspoon curry paste

INSTRUCTIONS:
a) In your instant pot, add one cup of water and the steamer rack.
b) Seal the lid and place the sweet potato on the rack, making sure that the release valve is in the right position.
c) Preheat the Instant Pot to high pressure for 15 minutes on manual. It will take a few minutes for the pressure to build up.
d) After the timer goes off, let the pressure drop naturally for 10 minutes. To discharge any remaining pressure, turn the release valve.
e) Once the float valve has fallen, remove the sweet potato by opening the lid.
f) When the sweet potato has cooled enough to handle, cut it in half and mash the flesh with a fork.
g) Top with pecans, blueberries, and chia seeds, then drizzle with maple syrup and almond butter.

17. Stuffed Sweet Potato on Arugula

Makes: 1

INGREDIENTS:
- ½ sweet potato, baked
- 2 eggs
- ½ cup micro arugula, chopped
- Salt and pepper
- Drizzle of Olive oil

INSTRUCTIONS:

a) Drizzle the greens lightly with olive oil and season with a pinch of salt.

b) Preheat a skillet or griddle over medium-high heat.

c) When the pan is heated, add the olive oil and cook for about 30 seconds before adding the sweet potato.

d) Cook until the edges begin to brown, then flip.

e) Take the sweet potato slices out of the skillet and set them straight on top of the prepared greens.

f) Then, in your skillet, crack the two eggs.

g) While the eggs are cooking, season them with salt and pepper.

h) For a little extra flavor, sprinkle on some herbs such as oregano or thyme, or crushed red pepper.

i) Place the eggs on top of the sweet potato slices.

j) Garnish with the greens you set aside.

18. Chiles Anchos Rellenos

4 servings

Ingredients
For the chiles
- 1 tablespoon oil
- 2 cups thinly sliced white onion
- 3 cloves garlic, peeled and smashed
- 2 tablespoons tamarind paste dissolved in 2 cups hot water
- 1 cup melao (cane syrup) or brown sugar
- 1/2 teaspoon dried leaf oregano
- 1/2 teaspoon dried thyme
- 1/2 teaspoon salt
- 8 medium to large ancho chiles, slit down one side, seeds removed

For the filling
- 4 cups Roasted-Garlic Sweet Potatoes
- Roasted Carrots
- 2 ounces goat cheese, grated
- Pinch salt
- 2 teaspoons extra-virgin olive oil

Directions

a) Prepare the chiles. Heat the oil over low to medium heat in a medium-sized saucepan. Add the onion and cook until it has browned slightly. Add the garlic and cook another minute.

b) Stir in the tamarind-flavored water, melao, oregano, thyme, and salt.

c) Add the chiles, cover, and cook at a bare simmer for 10 minutes. Remove the pan from the heat, uncover, and cool for at least 10 minutes.

d) Make the filling. While the chiles are cooling, combine the sweet potatoes and/or carrots and queso fresco or panela. Whisk together the salt, and oil and toss it with the vegetables.

e) Stuff and serve the chiles. Using a large slotted spoon, remove the chiles to a strainer and drain for 5 minutes.

f) Carefully spoon about 1/4 cup of the filling into each chile and put 2 on each of four plates. Spoon a little of the onions over each serving and top with the cheese. Serve at room temperature.

19. Sweet Potato and Carrot Tinga Tacos

Total Time-30 minutes

Ingredients
- 1/4 cup Water
- 1 cup Thinly sliced white onion
- 3 Garlic cloves, minced
- 2 1/2 cups Grated sweet potato
- 1 cup Grated carrot
- 1 can (14 oz.) Diced tomatoes
- 1 tsp. Mexican oregano (optional)
- 2 Chipotle peppers in adobo
- 1/2 cup Vegetable stock
- 1 Avocado, sliced
- 8 Tortillas

Directions
a) In a large sauté pan over medium-heat, add water and onion, cook for 3-4 minutes, until the onion is translucent and soft. Add the garlic and continue to cook, stirring for 1 minute.

b) Add sweet potato and carrot to the pan and cook for 5 min stirring often.

c) Sauce:

d) Place the diced tomatoes, vegetable stock, oregano, and chipotle peppers in the blender and process until smooth.

e) Add chipotle-tomato sauce to the pan and cook for 10-12 minutes, stirring occasionally, until the sweet potatoes and carrot are cooked through. If necessary, add more vegetable stock to the pan.

f) Serve on warm tortillas and top with avocado slices.

20. ROASTED ROOTS PIZZA

Ingredient

- All-purpose flour for dusting the pizza peel or olive oil for greasing the pizza tray
- 1 homemade dough
- 1/2 large garlic head
- 1/2 small sweet potatoes, peeled, halved lengthwise, and thinly sliced
- 1/2 small fennel bulb, halved, trimmed, and thinly sliced
- 1/2 small parsnips, peeled, halved lengthwise, and thinly sliced
- 1 tablespoon olive oil
- 1/2 teaspoon salt
- 4 ounces (1/4 pound) mozzarella, shredded
- 1 ounce Parmigiana, finely grated
- 1 tablespoon syrupy balsamic vinegar

DIRECTIONS

a) Wrap the unpeeled garlic cloves in a small aluminum foil packet and bake or grill directly over the heat for 40 minutes.

b) Meanwhile, toss the sweet potato, fennel, and parsnip in a large bowl with the olive oil and salt.

c) Pour the contents of the bowl onto a large baking sheet.

d) Place in the oven or over the unheated section of the grill and roast, turning occasionally, until soft and sweet, 15 to 20 minutes.

e) Transfer the garlic to a cutting board open the packet, taking care to mind the steam.

f) Increase the oven's or gas grill's temperature to 450°F.

g) Spread the shredded mozzarella over the prepared crust, leaving a 1/2-inch border at the edge. Top the cheese with all the vegetables squeeze the pulpy, soft garlic out of its papery hulls and onto the pie. Top with the grated Parmigiana.

h)

i) Slide the pizza from the peel to the hot stone or place the pizza on its tray or baking sheet either in the oven or over the unheated section of the grill. Bake or grill with the lid closed until the crust has turned golden brown and even darkened a bit on its bottom, until the cheese has melted and started to brown, 16 to minutes. Fresh dough may develop some air bubbles during the first 10 minutes; particularly at its edge pop these with a fork to assure an even crust.

j) Slide the peel back under the crust to take it off the hot stone or transfer the pizza on its tray or baking sheet to a wire rack. Set aside for 5 minutes. To keep the crust crunchy, you might want to transfer the pie from the peel, tray, or flour sheet right onto the wire rack to cool after a minute or so.

k) Once cooled a bit, drizzle the pie with the balsamic vinegar, then slice into wedges to serve.

21. Sweet potato latkes

Makes: 4 Servings

INGREDIENTS:
- 1¾ pounds Orange-fleshed sweet potatoes; peeled
- 1 Onion
- 5 Egg whites
- ½ teaspoon Salt
- ¼ teaspoon Ground white pepper
- ⅓ cup Flour
- Oil
- 1⅓ cup Applesauce; optional

INSTRUCTIONS:
a) Grate sweet potatoes and onion in food processor with grating disk or through large holes of hand grater. Transfer to large bowl. Beat egg whites lightly with salt and pepper and add to potato mixture. Mix well. Add flour and mix well.

b) Heat 2 tablespoons oil over medium heat in heavy nonstick 10- to 12-inch skillet. Fill ¼-cup measure with mixture, pressing to compact, and turn out in mound in skillet. Quickly repeat for 3 more latkes. Flatten each with back of spoon to form 2½- to 3-inch cake and press to compact. Cook 1- ½ minutes per side.

c) Remove to nonstick baking sheet with slotted spatula. Continue with remaining batter, adding a little more oil to pan and stirring batter for each batch.

d) Bake at 450 degrees F until golden brown, about 10 minutes. Turn over and bake 5 more minutes. Serve hot with applesauce if desired.

22. Daigaku imo

SERVES 2–4

- 1 sweet potatoes
- 3 tablespoons vegetable oil
- 5 tablespoons caster sugar
- ¼ teaspoon soy sauce

grated zest of 1 lime, plus the juice of ½ lime 1 teaspoon black sesame seeds

INSTRUCTIONS:

a) Wash the sweet potato thoroughly (don't peel it) and cut it into irregular wedges no larger than 3cm thick. Soak the wedges in cold water for 20–30 minutes to remove the excess starch, then dry completely with kitchen paper or a clean tea towel.

b) Place the oil, sugar, soy sauce, lime zest and juice in a deep frying pan over a low heat and stir. Add the potatoes to the pan, toss to coat in the sugar mixture, and increase the heat to medium. Place a lid on the pan and leave to heat until you hear it sizzling.

c) Turn the heat down to medium-low and cook for a further 2–3 minutes, then remove the lid and cook for another 10 minutes or so, turning the potatoes frequently to ensure they brown lightly on all sides. The potatoes are done when you can pierce them easily with a chopstick or butter knife.

d) When the potatoes are tender and nicely browned, turn off the heat and stir through the sesame seeds.

e) Leave to cool slightly, then enjoy them on their own or with vanilla ice cream.

23. **Quinoa muffin bites**

INGREDIENTS:
- 1 ½ cups prepared quinoa.
- 2 eggs, whisked.
- ½ cup sweet potato puree.
- ½ cup black beans.
- 1 tablespoon chopped cilantro.
- 1 teaspoons cumin.
- 1 teaspoon paprika.
- ½ teaspoons garlic powder.
- ½ teaspoons salt.
- ⅛ teaspoons black pepper.
- Cooking spray.

INSTRUCTIONS:

a) Pre-heat oven to 350° F. add all ingredients to a large bowl and mix till everything is integrated.

b) Spoon the mixture into the muffin tins utilizing a tablespoon, and pat down the top of each one. Bake up until cooked through and holding together about 15-20 minutes.

24. Turmeric Sweet Potato Patties

Makes: 10 patties

INGREDIENTS:
- ½ cup gram flour
- 1 sweet potato, peeled and diced
- ½ yellow or red onion, peeled and finely diced
- 1 tablespoon lemon juice
- Chopped fresh parsley or cilantro, for garnish
- 1 teaspoon turmeric powder
- 1 teaspoon ground coriander
- 1 teaspoon garam masala
- 3 tablespoons oil, divided
- 1 piece of ginger root, peeled and grated or minced
- 1 teaspoon cumin seeds
- 1 teaspoon red chile powder or cayenne
- 1 cup peas, fresh or frozen
- 1 green Thai, serrano, or cayenne chile, chopped
- 1 teaspoon coarse sea salt

INSTRUCTIONS:

a) Steam the potato for 7 minutes, or until soft.
b) Gently break it down with a potato masher.
c) Heat 2 tablespoons of the oil in a shallow frying pan over medium heat.
d) Add the cumin and cook for 30 seconds, or until it sizzles.
e) Add the onion, ginger root, turmeric, coriander, garam masala, and red chile powder.
f) Cook for another 3 minutes, or until soft.
g) Allow the mixture to cool.
h) Once the mixture has cooled, add it to the potatoes, along with the peas, green chiles, salt, gram flour, and lemon juice.
i) Mix thoroughly with your hands.
j) Shape the mixture into patties and place them on a baking sheet.
k) Heat the remaining 1 tablespoon of oil in a heavy pan over medium heat.
l) Cook the patties in batches for 3 minutes per side.
m) Serve, garnished with fresh parsley or cilantro.

25. **Sweet potato nachos**

Makes: 6

INGREDIENTS:
- 1 tablespoon olive oil
- ⅓ cup chopped tomato
- ⅓ cup chopped avocado
- 1 teaspoon chili powder
- 1 teaspoon garlic powder
- 3 sweet potatoes
- 1½ teaspoons paprika
- ⅓ cup reduced-fat shredded Cheddar cheese

INSTRUCTIONS:
a) Preheat oven to 425 degrees Fahrenheit. Coat the baking pans with nonstick cooking spray and cover them with foil.
b) Peel and thinly slice the sweet potatoes into 14-inch rounds.
c) Toss the rounds with olive oil, chili powder, garlic powder, and paprika.
d) Spread equally on the preheated pan and bake for 25 minutes, flipping halfway through the cooking time until crisp.
e) Remove the skillet from the oven and top the sweet potatoes with beans and cheese.
f) Bake for another 2 minutes until the cheese has melted.
g) Toss in the tomato and avocado. Serve.

26. Sweet potato Marshmallow bites

Makes: 6-8

INGREDIENTS:
- 4 sweet potatoes, peeled and sliced
- 2 tablespoons melted plant-based butter
- 1 teaspoon maple syrup
- Kosher salt
- 10-ounce bag of marshmallows
- ½ cup of pecan halves

INSTRUCTIONS:
a) Preheat the oven to 400 degrees Fahrenheit.
b) Toss sweet potatoes with melted plant-based butter and maple syrup on a baking sheet and arrange them in an even layer. Season with salt and pepper.
c) Bake until soft, about 20 minutes, flipping halfway through. Remove.
d) Top each sweet potato round with a marshmallow and broil for 5 minutes.
e) Serve immediately with a pecan half on top of each marshmallow.

27. Ceviche Peruano

Ingredients

- 2 medium potatoes
- 2 each sweet potatoes
- 1 red onion, cut into thin strips
- 1 cup fresh lime juice
- 1/2 stalk celery, sliced
- 1/4 cup lightly packed cilantro leaves
- 1 pinch ground cumin
- 1 clove garlic, minced
- 1 habanero pepper
- 1 pinch salt and freshly ground pepper
- 1-pound fresh tilapia, cut into 1/2-inch
- 1-pound medium shrimp - peeled,

Directions

a) Place the potatoes and sweet potatoes in a saucepan and cover with water. Place the sliced onion in a bowl of warm water.

b) Blend celery, cilantro, and cumin and stir in the garlic and habanero pepper. Season with salt and pepper, then stir in the diced tilapia and shrimp

c) To serve, peel the potatoes and cut into slices. Stir the onions into the fish mixture. Line serving bowls with lettuce leaves. Spoon the ceviche which consists of juice into the bowls and garnish with slices of potato.

28. Gingered sweet-potato fritters

Makes: 1 servings

INGREDIENTS:
- 1/2-pound sweet potato
- 1½ teaspoon Minced peeled fresh gingerroot
- 2 teaspoons Fresh lemon juice
- ¼ teaspoon Dried hot red pepper flakes
- ¼ teaspoon Salt
- 1 large Egg
- 5 tablespoons All-purpose flour
- Vegetable oil for deep-frying

INSTRUCTIONS:
a) Peel and grate coarse the sweet potato. In a food processor chop fine the grated sweet potato with the gingerroot, the lemon juice, the red pepper flakes, and the salt, add the egg and the flour, and blend the mixture well.

b) In a large saucepan heat 1½ inches of the oil over moderately high heat to 360F. on a deep-fat thermometer, drop tablespoons of the sweet-potato mixture into the oil in batches, and fry the fritters, turning them, for 2 minutes, or until they are golden.

c) Transfer the fritters to paper towels to drain.

BURGERS, WRAPS, AND SANDWICHES

29. Quinoa and Sweet Potato Burger

Makes: 6

Ingredients
- 3 medium sweet potatoes, baked
- 2 eggs
- 1 cup chickpea flour
- 1 teaspoon chili powder
- 1 tablespoon wholegrain Dijon mustard
- 1 tablespoon Walnut Butter or other Nut Butter
- juice of ½ lemon
- 1 pinch of sea salt
- 200 g quinoa
- peanut oil, for frying
- Horseradish sour cream
- 3 tablespoons finely grated horseradish
- 1¼ cups sour cream
- sea salt

To serve
- 6 burger buns, halved
- butter for the buns
- finely sliced red Asian shallots
- finely chopped chives

Directions

a) Split the potatoes lengthwise and use a spoon to scrape out the insides.

b) Blend the eggs in a food processor and blend in the sweet potatoes, chickpea flour, chili powder, mustard, Nut Butter, lemon juice, and salt. Add the quinoa.

c) Using a handful of the mixture at a time, form round patties.

d) In a mixing bowl, combine the salt, horseradish, and sour cream.

e) Over medium heat, grill the patties for a few minutes on both sides.

f) Butter the cut surfaces of the buns and rapidly grill them.

g) Place a burger on the bottom of each bun, and cover with horseradish sour cream, shallots, and chives.

30. Lentil rice burgers

Makes: 8 servings

Ingredients
- ¾ cup Lentils
- 1 Sweet potato
- 10 Fresh spinach leaves, shredded
- 1 cup fresh mushrooms, diced
- ¾ cup Bread crumbs
- 1 teaspoon Tarragon
- 1 teaspoon Garlic powder
- 1 teaspoon Parsley flakes
- ¾ cup Long grain rice

Directions
a) Cook rice till soft and slightly sticky, then add lentils.
b) Mince a cooked peeled sweet potato.
c) Combine the rice mixture, sweet potato, and all the other ingredients in a mixing bowl.
a) Refrigerate for 15 to 30 minutes. Form into patties and cook on an outdoor barbecue with a vegetable grill.
b) Be sure to oil or spray the pan with Pam to prevent the burgers from sticking.

31. Spicy Sweet Potato & Black Bean Taquitos

Makes: 3

INGREDIENTS:
- 1 medium potato roasted sweet potato
- 1/4 cup black beans, cooked
- 3 4" corn tortillas
- 1 tablespoon plant-based butter
- 1/4 teaspoon onion powder
- 1/4 teaspoon garlic powder
- 1/2 teaspoon chili powder
- 1 teaspoon chili flakes
- 1 tablespoon nutritional yeast
- 1/4 teaspoon paprika
- 1/2 teaspoon cumin
- 1 teaspoon kosher salt

INSTRUCTIONS:
a) Turn on your air fryer for 4 minutes at 400 °F.
b) In a bowl, scoop the sweet potato using a fork, then mash it together with plant-based butter.
c) Stir the nutritional yeast and all of the spices until a smooth consistency is achieved.
d) Wrap tortillas in a damp paper towel and microwave for 30 seconds to make them less likely to tear while wrapping.
e) Using a plate, add about 1 teaspoon of vegetable broth. Place a tortilla on the plate and rub to coat one side with broth.
f) To the dry side of the tortilla, add ⅓ of the mixture near its edge and 1½ tablespoon of beans. Press the beans into the potatoes to keep them from falling out.
g) Roll into a taquito by picking up the filled edge and turning it over. Make sure to roll tightly and carefully to avoid the tortilla from ripping.

h) Place the seam down into the basket of the air fryer.

i) Repeat filling all the remaining servings of tortillas until all taquitos are made.

j) Cook for 10 minutes in the fryer until the shells are completely crispy.

k) Garnish with guacamole, salsa, or plant-based crema.

MAIN COURSE

32. Spicy Chicken Quarters With Sweet Potatoes

Makes: 4

INGREDIENTS:
- ½ teaspoon black pepper
- 2 tablespoons olive oil
- 2 sweet potatoes, peeled and cubed
- 1 tablespoon cornstarch
- ½ teaspoon cayenne pepper
- 1 tablespoon water
- 1 teaspoon chili powder
- Fresh cilantro leaves
- ¼ teaspoon ground cinnamon
- 1 tablespoon light brown sugar
- 1 teaspoon kosher salt
- ¾ cup unsalted chicken stock
- 4 chicken leg quarters, skinned

INSTRUCTIONS:
a) In a Crockpot, arrange the sweet potatoes in a layer and season with salt and black pepper.
b) In a mixing bowl, combine the brown sugar, chili powder, cayenne pepper, and cinnamon.
c) Rub the spice mixture all over the chicken.
d) Heat the oil in a nonstick skillet over moderate heat.
e) Brown the chicken on both sides, 2 to 3 minutes per side.
f) Remove the chicken from the skillet, reserving the drippings in the skillet.
g) Place the chicken in a single layer, with the pieces slightly overlapping, on the sweet potatoes in the Crockpot.
h) Add the stock to the conserved drippings in the skillet and Cook on low for about 2 minutes, swirling and scraping to release the browned bits from the bottom of the skillet.

i) Pour the chicken stock mixture over it.
j) Cook on low heat for 4 hours.
k) Reserve the cooking liquid in the Crockpot and transfer the chicken and sweet potatoes to a serving plate.
l) Skim and discard the fat from the cooking liquid, then transfer it to a medium pot.
m) Bring to a boil on high heat.
n) Combine the cornstarch and water; stir the cornstarch mixture into the boiling cooking liquid and Cook on low, whisking constantly, until thickened, about 1 minute.
o) Serve the sauce alongside the chicken and sweet potatoes, Garnish as desired.

33. Garlic Florentine Sweet Potatoes

Makes: 4 servings

INGREDIENTS:
- 4 sweet potatoes
- 2, 10-ounce packages of spinach
- 1 tablespoon olive oil
- 1 shallot, minced
- 2 cloves garlic, minced
- 6 sun-dried tomatoes, diced
- ¼ teaspoon salt
- ¼ teaspoon black pepper
- ¼ teaspoon red pepper flakes
- ½ cup part-skim ricotta cheese

INSTRUCTIONS:
a) Get the oven ready by preheating it to 400 degrees Fahrenheit.
b) Place the sweet potatoes on a prepared baking sheet after piercing them with a fork.
c) Bake for 45-60 minutes until the potatoes are cooked. Allow time for cooling.
d) Split the potatoes along the middle with a knife and fluff the potato flesh with a fork, then set aside.
e) In a pan, heat the oil over moderate heat. Cook for 3 minutes until shallots are softened.
f) Cook for another 30 seconds until the garlic is aromatic.
g) Combine the drained spinach, tomatoes, salt, black pepper, and red pepper flakes. Cook for another 2 minutes.
h) Remove from the heat and reserve to cool.
i) Incorporate the ricotta cheese into the spinach mixture.
j) Serve the spinach mixture on top of the divided sweet potatoes.

34. Risotto with Green Beans and Sweet Potatoes

Makes: 8

INGREDIENTS:
- 1 large sweet potato
- 5 garlic cloves, minced
- 2 cups short-grain brown rice
- 1 teaspoon dried thyme leaves
- 7 cups low-sodium vegetable broth
- 2 cups green beans, cut in half crosswise
- 3 tablespoons unsalted butter
- ½ cup Parmesan cheese

INSTRUCTIONS:
a) In a 6-quart slow cooker, mix the sweet potato, garlic, rice, thyme, and broth.
b) Cover and cook over low heat for 3 to 4 hours.
c) Mix in the green beans.
d) Cover and cook over low heat for 37 minutes.
e) Stir in the butter and cheese. Cover and cook at low for 20 minutes, then stir and serve.

35. **Baked Salmon and Sweet Potatoes**

Servings: 4 servings

Ingredients

- 4 salmon fillets, skin removed
- 4 medium sized sweet potatoes, peeled and cut into 1-inch thick
- 1 cup broccoli florets
- 4 Tablespoons pure honey (or maple syrup)
- 2 Tablespoons orange marmalade/jam
- 1 1-inch fresh ginger knob, grated
- 1 teaspoons Dijon mustard
- 1 Tablespoons sesame seeds, toasted
- 2 Tablespoons unsalted butter, melted
- 2 teaspoons sesame oil
- Salt and pepper to taste
- Spring onions/scallions, freshly chopped

INSTRUCTIONS:

a) Preheat the oven to 400F. Grease the baking pan with melted unsalted butter.

b) Place the sliced sweet potatoes and broccoli florets in the pan. Lightly season with salt, pepper and a teaspoons of sesame oil. Make sure the vegetables are lightly coated with sesame oil.

c) Bake the potatoes and broccoli for 10-12 minutes.

d) While the vegetables are still in the oven, prepare the sweet glaze. In a mixing bowl, add in the honey (or maple syrup), orange jam, grated ginger, sesame oil and mustard.

e) Carefully remove the baking pan from the oven and spread the vegetables to the side to make room for the fish.

f) Lightly season the salmon with salt and pepper.

g) Place the salmon fillets in the middle of the baking pan and pour in the sweet glaze over the salmon and the vegetables.

h) Return the pan to the oven and cook for an additional 8-10 minutes or until the salmon is fork tender.

i) Transfer the salmon, sweet potatoes and broccoli to a nice serving platter. Garnish with sesame seeds and spring onions.

36. Salmon Teriyaki with Vegetables

Servings: 4 servings

Ingredients

- 4 salmon fillets, skin and pin bones removed
- 1 large sweet potato (or simply potato), cut into bite-size pieces
- 1 large carrot, cut into bite-size pieces
- 1 large white onion, cut into wedges
- 3 large bell peppers (green, red and yellow), chopped
- 2 cups broccoli florets (can be replaced with asparagus)
- 2 Tablespoons extra virgin olive oil
- Salt and pepper to taste
- Spring onions, finely chopped
- Teriyaki sauce
- 1 cup water
- 3 Tablespoons soy sauce
- 1 Tablespoons garlic, minced
- 3 Tablespoons brown sugar
- 2 Tablespoons pure honey
- 2 Tablespoons corn starch (dissolved in 3 Tablespoons water)
- ½ Tablespoons toasted sesame seeds

INSTRUCTIONS:

a) In a small skillet, whisk soy sauce, ginger, garlic, sugar, honey and water over low heat. Stir continuously until the mixture simmers slowly. Stir in the cornstarch water and wait until the mixture thickens. Add in the sesame seeds and set aside.

b) Grease a large baking dish with unsalted butter or cooking spray. Preheat the oven to 400F.

c) In a large bowl, dump all the vegetables and drizzle with olive oil. Mix well until the vegetables are well coated with oil. Season with freshly cracked pepper and a bit of salt. Transfer the vegetables to the baking dish. Scatter the vegetables to the sides and leave some space in the center of the baking dish.

d) Place the salmon in the center of the baking dish. Pour in 2/3 of the teriyaki sauce to the vegetables and salmon.

e) Bake the salmon for 15-20 minutes.

f) Transfer the baked salmon and roasted vegetables to a nice serving platter. Pour in the remaining teriyaki sauce and garnish with chopped spring onions.

37. Salmon with sweet potatoes and beans

This dish is fast, very good and simple especially for the evening.

Ingrédients:
- For two persons
- 2 salmon patties
- 1 large sweet potato (very large)
- 200 g green beans
- Lemon juicedill (thesenare romantic herbs, it goes well with salmon, but if you does not matter 2 tablespoons of olive oïl for cooking salmon)
- Butter (1 tablespoon)
- 5cl of oïl (any) for cooking sweet potato
- Salt , papper

Preparation:
a) Start by removing the inedile ends of the beans and cut them into pieces about 3 cm long. Then cook with steam for 10 minutes. Then put olive oïl in a pan but it may be optional. I did it for this case though but cooking steam is enough. Reserve the beans

b) Then put the olive oïl in a pan. Add salmon steaks. And cook for a few minutes. Both sides must be colored. Salt each face. Reserve and sprinkle with dill.

c) Peel the sweet potato. And cut into thick slices. Then cut each puck in half (half circles).

d) Heat the oïl. Cook sweet potato pieces over medium heat. It must be cooked and colored on each side. Remove and salt.

e) Enjoy the salmon with the fried sweet potatoes that are melting Inside and the beans in butter.

f) You can eat a drizzle of lemon juice on the salmon.

38. Matcha Steamed Cod

Makes: 4 servings

INGREDIENTS
- 2 cups julienned peeled sweet potato
- 1 pound cod, cut into 4 pieces
- 2 teaspoons matcha powder
- 4 tablespoons unsalted butter
- 8 sprigs of fresh thyme
- 4 slices fresh lemon
- 1 teaspoon kosher salt

INSTRUCTIONS:
a) Preheat oven to 425 degrees F. Take 4 sheets of parchment paper, each about 12 by 16 inches, in half and then unfold to make a crease.

b) Place a pile of sweet potato strips on one side of each piece of parchment and top each with a piece of cod.

c) Sprinkle each piece of fish with 1 teaspoon of matcha, then top each with 1 tablespoon of butter, 2 sprigs thyme, and a slice of lemon; season with salt.

d) Fold over parchment paper to enclose filling and crimp edges to seal and form a crescent-shaped packet.

e) Transfer to a baking sheet and bake for 20 minutes. Remove packets from the oven and allow them to rest for 5 to 10 minutes before opening.

39. Sweet Potato Marshmallow Casserole

Makes: 10 Servings

INGREDIENTS:
- 4 ½ pounds sweet potatoes
- 1 cup granulated sugar
- ½ cup vegan butter softened
- ¼ cup plant-based milk
- 1 teaspoon vanilla extract
- ¼ teaspoon salt
- 1 ¼ cups cornflakes cereal, crushed
- ¼ cup chopped pecans
- 1 tablespoon brown sugar
- 1 tablespoon vegan butter, melted
- 1½ cups miniature marshmallows

INSTRUCTIONS:
a) Preheat the oven to 425 degrees Fahrenheit.
b) Roast sweet potatoes for 1 hour or until soft.
c) Slice sweet potatoes in half and scoop out the insides into a mixing dish.
d) Using an electric mixer, beat the mashed sweet potatoes, granulated sugar, and the following 5 ingredients until smooth.
e) Spoon the potato mixture into an 11 x 7-inch baking dish that has been greased.
f) In a mixing bowl, combine cornflakes cereal and the next three ingredients.
g) Sprinkle in diagonal rows 2 inches apart over the dish.
h) Bake for 30 minutes.
i) In between rows of cornflakes, sprinkle marshmallows; bake for 10 minutes.

40. Cold roast duck with vegetables

Makes: 4 Servings

INGREDIENTS:
- 1 cup Sweet potatoes
- 1 cup Carrots
- 1 cup Cucumber
- 1 cup Chinese white turnip
- 1 Green pepper
- 1 cup Chinese cabbage (up to)
- 1 cup Sugar
- 1 cup Vinegar
- 1 tablespoon Catsup
- 1 tablespoon Oil
- ½ teaspoon Salt
- ½ teaspoon Hot sauce
- 3 drops Sesame oil; more or less
- 1 pinch Cinnamon
- 1 dash Pepper
- 1 Head lettuce (up to)
- 2 pounds Roast duck

INSTRUCTIONS:
a) Peel and shred sweet potatoes, carrots, cucumber and Chinese white turnip. Shred green pepper and Chinese cabbage.
b) Combine sugar, vinegar, catsup, oil, salt, hot sauce, sesame oil, cinnamon and pepper. Add to shredded vegetables and toss well. Refrigerate, covered, 24 hours.
c) Toss vegetables again and refrigerate, covered, 24 hours more. Drain, discarding marinade.
d) Shred lettuce and arrange on a serving platter. Top with drained vegetables.
e) Bone and shred roast duck. Arrange over vegetables and serve.

41. Buffalo Tempeh Harvest Bowls

Makes: 2

INGREDIENTS:
- 8oz tempeh
- 1oz maple syrup
- 1.5oz hot sauce
- 1 teaspoon Dijon mustard
- 3 garlic cloves
- 4oz mixed greens
- 1 sweet potato
- 4 tablespoons vegetable broth, divided
- 2 teaspoons vegetable broth
- 1 medium apple
- 1/2oz red wine vinegar
- 1/4 cup soy free vegenaise
- 1/3 cup walnuts
- Salt and pepper

INSTRUCTIONS:
a) Preheat the oven to 400 °F.
b) In a medium bowl, whisk the hot sauce, and 1 tablespoon vegetable broth to prepare Buffalo sauce.
c) Slice the tempeh into 1/4-inch thick strips and toss with the Buffalo sauce to coat.
d) Remove the garlic cloves and cut the sweet potato half lengthwise, then into 4-5 wedges.
e) Line a baking sheet using foil or parchment paper. Remove the tempeh from the bowl, gently shake to remove any excess sauce, and place on a baking sheet lined with parchment paper.
f) Toss the garlic cloves, sweet potato wedges, and 1 teaspoon vegetable broth on the opposite side of the baking sheet.
g) Sprinkle salt and pepper over everything on the baking sheet.

h) Bake for at least 22 to 24 minutes or until the Buffalo tempeh is crispy and the sweet potatoes are tender.

i) Mix and combine all of the ingredients for the roasted garlic dressing in a mixing bowl.

j) Mash the roasted garlic cloves in a small bowl. Whisk in the remaining red wine vinegar, Vegenaise, Dijon mustard, and a pinch of salt and pepper to make the roasted garlic dressing.

k) Toss the apple salad with the Buffalo tempeh and mixed greens to combine. Add roasted sweet potato wedges and candied walnuts on top. Drizzle with roasted garlic dressing.

SOUPS AND CURRIES

42. **Crockpot chicken soup**

Makes: 8

INGREDIENTS
- 2 tablespoons chopped chives
- 3 pounds of fried chicken
- ½ teaspoon tarragon, chopped
- 2 cups of chopped tomatoes
- 1 cup of corn kernels
- ½ cup green onions, chopped
- 1 teaspoon basil, chopped
- ½ cup shelled peas
- 6 cups defatted chicken broth
- ½ cup diced sweet potatoes
- ½ cup dry sherry

INSTRUCTIONS:

a) Cook the chicken pieces in sherry for roughly 10 minutes in a saucepan and then add the tomatoes, corn, green onions, and sweet potatoes.

b) Cook for 5 minutes after adding the peas, spring onions, basil, tarragon, and chili.

c) Add the chicken pieces, water, and broth and transfer to a crockpot.

d) Cook on low for 1 hour.

43. **Thai Coconut-Curry Flounder**

Makes: 6

INGREDIENTS:
- 2 tablespoons canola oil
- 1 cup uncooked brown jasmine rice
- 1 cup canned light coconut milk
- ¼ cup thinly sliced fresh basil
- 1½ cups water
- 1 cup chopped green bell pepper
- 2 tablespoons minced garlic
- 2½ tablespoons Thai red curry paste
- 1½ pounds skinless flounder fillets
- 2 sweet potatoes, peeled and cubed
- 14½-ounce can of diced tomatoes, undrained
- ¼ teaspoon kosher salt

INSTRUCTIONS:

a) In a microwavable bowl, microwave the sweet potatoes on HIGH for 5 to 6 minutes, stopping to stir after 3 minutes.

b) In a 6-quart Crockpot, sprinkle the rice with the oil and stir to coat evenly.

c) Stir in the tomatoes, water, bell pepper, garlic, and sweet potatoes.

d) Cook, covered, on HIGH for 3 hours.

e) Incorporate the coconut milk and curry paste into the rice mixture gently.

f) Cook, covered, on HIGH for 15 minutes, or until the liquid is mostly absorbed.

g) Place the fish on top of the rice mixture and season with salt.

h) Cook, covered, on HIGH for 20 minutes, or until the salmon flakes readily with a fork.

i) Serve the fish with the rice mixture and sprinkle with basil evenly.

44. Crockpot Carrot ginger soup

Makes: 6

INGREDIENTS
- Pinch Kosher salt and ground black pepper
- 3 garlic cloves
- ¼ cup mint leaves
- 1 teaspoon smoked paprika
- ⅓ cup heavy cream
- 1 sweet onion, chopped
- 2 pounds carrots, peeled and chopped
- ⅓ cup coriander leaves
- 2 bay leaves
- 2 tablespoons lime juice
- 1 sweet potato, peeled and chopped
- 6 cups vegetable broth
- 1 piece of ginger, peeled and sliced
- ¼ teaspoon smoked paprika

INSTRUCTIONS:
a) Using a Crockpot, mix the carrots, sweet potatoes, onion, garlic, ginger, paprika, bay leaves, and broth. Season with salt and pepper.
b) Cook on low for 1 hour.
c) Add lime juice, mint, and coriander.
d) Remove the bay leaves and then puree them using a blender.
e) Serve with a dollop of cream.

45. Bouillon Soup

Makes: 6 Servings

INGREDIENTS
- 2 pounds beef shanks, rinsed and patted dry
- 4 soft blue crabs optional
- 2 tablespoons lime juice fresh
- ½ teaspoon ground black pepper
- 1 tablespoon salt
- 2 tablespoons parsley chopped
- 2 scallions finely chopped
- 1 sprig thyme
- 3 tablespoons garlic finely chopped
- 2 ¼ cups all-purpose flour
- 1 cup water
- 1 teaspoon salt
- 1 teaspoon black pepper ground
- ¼ teaspoon sweet paprika
- 2 tablespoons olive oil
- 1 white onion chopped
- 1 green bell pepper chopped
- 2 tomatoes chopped
- 2 malanga or Yautia. peeled and cubed
- 1 green plantain peeled and sliced
- 4 cups spinach well packed
- 1 chayote peeled and cubed
- 2 carrots peeled and cut into slices
- 2 parsnips peeled and cut into slices
- 2 potatoes peeled and cubed
- 2 medium white sweet potatoes peeled and cubed
- 2 tablespoons beef bouillon powder
- Pinch garlic powder to taste
- Pinch salt to taste

- Pinch pepper to taste
- ½ of a hot pepper or ¼ teaspoon of hot sauce

INSTRUCTIONS

a) Marinate the meat overnight in a bowl with the lime juice, parsley, salt, black pepper, garlic, scallions, and thyme.
b) Remove, and boil the meat, gradually add water.
c) Combine the flour, water, salt, pepper, and sweet paprika in a bowl.
d) Form dumplings with a spoon or your hands. Place aside.
e) If you're using blue crabs, clean them, take off the shell, and chop them in half along the middle.
f) Place oil, onions, and green peppers along with them blue crabs in a sizable stockpot and heat over medium heat for two to three minutes.
g) Add the parsnip, carrot, tomatoes, spinach, and chayote. Cook for 4 to 5 minutes.
h) Add 8 cups of water, cover, and bring to a boil.
i) Allow vegetables to simmer for 7 to 8 minutes.
j) Add the other ingredients, including the meat and the dumplings.
k) Cover loosely and allow to simmer for 25 to 30 minutes, or until all ingredients, including the dumplings, are thoroughly cooked.
l) Serve hot.

46. Curried Lentils with Sweet Potatoes and Chickpeas

INGREDIENTS:
- ¼ cup coconut oil
- 1 large red onion, diced
- Salt to taste
- 2 tablespoons curry powder
- 2 teaspoons cumin powder
- 2 teaspoons mustard seed
- 1 teaspoon ground coriander
- 8 ounces brown lentils
- 3 medium sweet potatoes
- 4 cups Chicken Bone Broth (2 cartons)
- 1 (28-oz) can fire-roasted diced tomatoes
- 1 (28-oz) can chickpeas, drained
- Fresh chopped parsley for garnishing

INSTRUCTIONS:

a) Heat coconut oil over medium heat in a large saucepan for about 1 minute.

b) Add onion and a pinch of salt. Sauté until onions are translucent.

c) Add curry powder, cumin, mustard seed, and coriander and cook for 1 minute, stirring often.

d) Stir in lentils, sweet potatoes, broth, and tomatoes. Bring to a boil and let it simmer for 25 minutes, covered, or until the lentils and sweet potatoes are tender.

e) Stir in chickpeas and cook until they are heated through, about 2 minutes.

f) Dish and garnish with chopped parsley. Enjoy!

47. Mexican Beef And Sweet Potato Broth Soup

INGREDIENTS:
- 1 Tablespoon refined avocado oil or olive oil
- 1-pound lean stew beef
- 1 teaspoon kosher salt
- 1 cup chopped onion
- 1 teaspoon minced garlic
- 1 cup chopped sweet bell pepper
- 2 cups sweet potato, peeled and chopped
- 1 teaspoon chili powder
- 1 teaspoon dried oregano
- 1 teaspoon ground cumin
- 14 ounces of red salsa
- Chicken Broth, 2 cups
- 2 teaspoons lime juice
- ⅓ cup chopped cilantro
- Kosher salt to taste
- Ground black pepper to taste

INSTRUCTIONS:
a) Heat a large cast iron pan over high heat.
b) Add stew beef and sprinkle with salt. Stir beef until browned, 5 minutes. With a slotted spoon, remove the meat, and transfer it to a plate. Set aside.
c) Place onion, garlic, and bell pepper in the pan over medium-high heat stirring occasionally until onion and garlic are fragrant and peppers are tender or about 5 minutes.
d) Add the sweet potato, chili powder, oregano, cumin, broth, and salsa. Mix thoroughly. Bring to a boil. Then, cover and simmer for 30 minutes or until sweet potatoes are fork-tender.
e) Stir in lime juice, cilantro, salt, and pepper. Allow to heat through over low heat, about 4 minutes.

f) Ladle the Broth Soup into prepared jars, either pints or quarts, leaving 1-inch headspace.

g) Seal with 2-part canning lids to finger tight.

h) Process the jars in your pre-heated pressure canner for 40 minutes.

i) When the Processing time: is complete, turn off the heat and allow the canner to come to room temperature naturally.

j) When cool, remove the jars from the canner and check the seals.

48. Sweet potato and Tequila soup

Makes: 4 Servings

INGREDIENTS:
- 3 medium Sweet potatoes
- 4 tablespoons Tequila
- ¼ cup Unsalted butter; room temp.
- Fresh grated nutmeg to taste
- ½ teaspoon Salt
- Fresh ground white pepper to taste

INSTRUCTIONS:

a) Scrub unpeeled sweet potatoes, cut in large chunks and cook in lightly salted boiling water until tender. Then pour off water, cover pan and let potatoes 'fluff' about 5 minutes.

b) Quickly peel potatoes, add 2 tablespoons tequila, butter and nutmeg. Beat with an electric mixer or process in a food processor until smooth.

c) Taste and add salt, white pepper and 2 more tablespoons tequila, if desired. Serve warm. Makes 4 to 6 servings.

49. Red Bean Stew from Jamaica

Makes: 4 servings

INGREDIENTS
- 1 yellow onion, chopped
- 2 carrots, cut into slices
- ½ cup water
- 13.5-ounce can of coconut milk
- 2 garlic cloves, minced
- ¼ teaspoon black pepper
- 1 sweet potato, peeled and diced
- 3 cups cooked dark red kidney beans, drained and rinsed
- 1 tablespoon olive oil
- 1 teaspoon hot or mild curry powder
- 1 teaspoon dried thyme
- ¼ teaspoon ground allspice
- ½ teaspoon Low-Sodium Salt
- 14.5-ounce can of diced tomatoes, drained

INSTRUCTIONS

a) Heat the oil in a saucepan and cook the onion and carrots, for about 4 minutes.

b) Add garlic, sweet potato, and red pepper followed by kidney beans, tomatoes, curry powder, thyme, allspice, salt, and black pepper.

c) Stir in the water, and simmer, covered, for 30 minutes.

d) Stir in the coconut milk right at the end.

50. Chicken Soup

Preparation Time: 25 minutes
Cooking Time: 1 hour 15 minutes
Makes: 6 servings

INGREDIENTS
- 1½ -2 pounds chicken, cut into chunks
- 10 cups water 2 ½ liters
- 1 pounds pumpkin can use 1 butternut squash, chopped
- 2 potatoes Irish or sweet potatoes, chopped
- 1 Chocho chopped
- 2 carrots chopped
- 2 scallion chopped
- 6 sprigs thyme
- Scotch bonnet
- 8 pimento berries

FOR THE DUMPLING AND SPINNERS
- 2 cups of gluten-free flour 260g
- ½ cup water
- ½ teaspoon pink salt

INSTRUCTIONS
a) Bring a stock pot of water to a boil.
b) Add the chicken, half of the pumpkin or squash, and the pimento berries.
c) Boil the mixture for 30 minutes with the lid on, or until the chicken is cooked and the squash or pumpkin is soft.
d) Use a fork to mash the pumpkin or squash.
e) To make your dumplings, combine the flour and pink salt in a medium bowl, and then gradually add the water.
f) Combine the water and flour to form a dough ball.
g) Take a tiny bit of dough and roll it into the palm of your hands.

h) Form the doughball into discs to create dumplings that are typically formed.

i) Gently place each spinner and dumpling into the simmering broth.

j) Add the remaining pumpkin or squash, scallion, Chocho, potatoes, carrots, thyme, homemade cock soup blend, and scotch bonnet.

k) Cover the pot, and let the soup simmer for 45 minutes or until it thickens.

51. Corn Soup

Preparation Time: 10 minutes
Cooking Time: 1 hour 35 minutes
Makes: 6 Servings

INGREDIENTS:
- 1½ pounds of Salted Pigtails cut into pieces and boiled
- 1 ¼ cups Yellow Split Peas, washed
- 5 ¼ cups Water
- 4 cloves Garlic, crushed
- 2 tablespoons Coconut Oil
- 6 sprigs of Fresh Thyme
- 1 Onion, diced
- 2 stalks of Celery, diced
- ¼ cup Chopped Fresh Parsley
- 3 Scallions, chopped
- 3 Pimiento Peppers, diced
- 2 Red Bird's Eye Chili Pepper
- 3 tablespoons Chopped Cilantro Leaves
- ¼ teaspoon Freshly Ground Black Pepper
- 2 cups Diced Pumpkins
- 2 cups Diced Sweet Potatoes
- 2 cups Chicken Stock
- 1½ cups Coconut Milk
- 2 Carrots, diced
- 4 Corn cut into pieces
- 1 can Creamed Corn
- 1 cup Frozen Corn
- 1 cup All-Purpose Flour
- 1 pinch Salt

INSTRUCTIONS:

a) Combine the boiled pigtails with the Yellow Split Peas and Garlic and bring to a boil.

b) Simmer for 35-40 minutes or until the peas are tender.

c) Heat the Coconut Oil over a medium flame, then add the Onion, Scallions, Fresh Thyme, Pimiento Peppers, Cilantro Leaves, Fresh Parsley, Red Bird's Eye Chili Pepper, Celery, and Freshly Ground Black Pepper. Cook for about 4-5 minutes.

d) Add the Sweet Potatoes, Pumpkins, and Carrots and stir well. Then add the Chicken Stock and bring it to a boil for about 25 minutes.

e) Add the peas/pigtail to the soup pot, and stir well.

f) Add the Coconut Milk, Frozen Corn, and Creamed Corn.

g) Simmer for another 20 minutes.

h) Place the Water, All-Purpose Flour, and Salt in a bowl and knead to form a soft dough. Let the dough rest for about 5 minutes.

i) Divide into 3 smaller balls and roll each part out to form a thick straw, cylinder.

j) Cut into bite-size pieces, and add to the boiling soup.

k) Add the cut pieces of Corn, and cook for about 5 minutes.

52. Salmon Vegetable Chowder

Servings: 4 servings

INGREDIENTS:
- 2 salmon fillets, skin removed and cut into bite-size pieces
- 1 ½ cups white onion, finely chopped
- 1 ½ cups sweet potato, peeled and diced
- 1 cup broccoli florets, cut into small pieces
- 3 cups chicken broth
- 2 cups whole milk
- 2 Tablespoons all-purpose flour
- 1 teaspoon dried thyme
- 3 Tablespoons unsalted butter
- 1 bay leaf
- Salt and pepper to taste
- Flat parsley, finely chopped

INSTRUCTIONS:
a) Cook chopped onion in unsalted butter until translucent. Stir in flour and mix well with the butter and onion. Pour in chicken broth and milk, then add sweet potato cubes, bay leaf and thyme.
b) Let the mixture simmer for 5-10 minutes while stirring occasionally.
c) Add the salmon and broccoli florets. Then, cook for 5-8 minutes.
d) Season with salt and pepper and adjust the taste when necessary.
e) Transfer to small individual bowls and garnish with chopped parsley.

53. Ground bison and vegetable stew

Servings: 5-6

Ingredients
- 1 lb. ground bison
- 1-2 Tablespoons avocado oil
- 3 large carrots (2 cups), chopped
- 3 celery stalks (1 cup), sliced
- 2 large white sweet potatoes (2 cups), chopped
- 1/2 teaspoons salt
- 2 teaspoons turmeric
- 3 cups chicken broth
- 1 1/2 cups butternut squash, pureed
- 3 cups kale, chopped
- Fresh parsley, topping (optional)

Directions
a) Heat a large pan over medium heat and add the ground bison, breaking into pieces. Once the meat has finished cooking, remove from the pan and set to the side.

b) Heat the avocado oil in a large stock pot on medium heat. Once hot, add the chopped carrots and celery. Sauté for about 8 minutes.

c) Add the white sweet potatoes, salt and turmeric and combine ingredients. Continue cooking the ingredients over medium heat, stirring periodically, for another 10 minutes or until the vegetables have softened a bit.

d) Add in the broth, pureed butternut squash, kale, and bison. Stir all ingredients together and set to low-medium heat, letting the stew simmer for roughly 30 minutes.

e) Once the stew is ready, serve warm and top with fresh parsley if desired.

54. Coconut Beef Curry

SERVINGS: 4

INGREDIENTS:
- 1 ½ lbs. beef, cut into chunks
- ½ cup basil, sliced
- 2 Tablespoons brown sugar
- 2 Tablespoons fish sauce
- ¼ cup chicken stock
- ¾ cup coconut milk
- 2 Tablespoons curry paste
- 1 onion, sliced
- 1 bell pepper, sliced
- 1 sweet potato

INSTRUCTIONS:

a) In the instant pot, combine all ingredients except basil and stir well.

b) Cook on high for 15 minutes after sealing the pot with a lid.

c) Allow the pressure to naturally release before opening the lid.

d) Add the basil and mix thoroughly.

e) Serve.

55. Sweet potato and pumpkin soup

Makes 4 to 6 servings

INGREDIENTS:
- 1 small pumpkin (about 2 pounds)
- 1 teaspoon extra-virgin olive oil
- 5 cups vegetable stock, homemade or store-bought
- 1 (2-inch) cinnamon stick
- ½ teaspoon coarse sea salt
- 2 sweet potatoes (about 1½ pounds total), peeled and cut into 1-inch pieces
- 1 cup Creamed Cashews
- Freshly ground white pepper

INSTRUCTIONS:

a) Preheat the oven to 275°F. Line a small, rimmed baking sheet with parchment paper.

b) Cut the top off the pumpkin and scoop out the seeds. (It is fine if the seeds have some remnants of squash on them.) Put the seeds in a small bowl, drizzle with the oil, and toss until evenly coated.

c) Spread the seeds in a single layer on the lined baking sheet and bake for about 15 minutes, until lightly browned, stirring every 5 minutes for even cooking. Set aside.

d) Meanwhile, peel the pumpkin and cut it into 1-inch pieces. Put the stock, cinnamon stick, and salt in a large saucepan over medium heat and bring to a simmer. Cook for 5 minutes, then add the pumpkin and sweet potatoes. Increase the heat to high and bring to a boil.

e) Immediately decrease the heat to medium-low, cover, and simmer, stirring occasionally, until the vegetables are fork-tender, about 35 minutes. Stir in the cashew cream.

f) Using a standard blender and working in batches, or using an immersion blender, blend the soup until smooth. Pour the soup back into the saucepan and cook, over medium-low heat, stirring occasionally, until warmed through.

g) If necessary, thin with water so the soup pours easily from a spoon. Season with salt and pepper to taste. Serve garnished with the toasted pumpkin seeds.

56. Thai Sweet Potato Curry

Makes: 4-5

INGREDIENTS:
- Oil: 1 tablespoon
- Shallots: 2, thinly sliced
- Sweet potatoes: 2 (peeled and cubed)
- Fresh baby spinach: 3-4 cups
- Curry paste: 2-3 tablespoons
- Regular coconut milk: 1 (14 ounces)
- Broth or water: ½- 1 cup
- Peanuts and cilantro: ½ cup (chopped)
- Soy sauce: to taste

INSTRUCTIONS:
a) Garlic, shallots, and ginger should all be roasted.
b) In a food processor, mix all of the ingredients and some spices, lemongrass paste, and cilantro.
c) Heat the oil to a medium-high temperature.
d) Stir in the shallots and sweet potatoes to coat them in oil.
e) Stir in the curry paste until it is well mixed.
f) Add the spinach until it is fully wilted.
g) Add peanut/cilantro mixture, reserving some for garnishing.
h) Add soy sauce.
i) Serve with the remaining peanuts/cilantro on top of the rice.

57. Thai Curry Hot Pot

Makes: 8-10

INGREDIENTS:
HOT POT BROTH INGREDIENTS:
- Olive oil: 1 tablespoon
- Garlic cloves: 5, minced
- Fresh ginger: 1 inch (cut into thick slices)
- Kitchen basics vegetable stock: 8 cups
- Coconut milk: 3 cans (15 ounces)
- Thai Kitchen red curry paste: 4-6 tablespoons (to taste)

HOT POT DIPPERS AND TOPPING INGREDIENTS:
- Crispy tofu
- Noodles / rice
- Sliced bell peppers, sweet potatoes, broccoli, carrots, onions, peas, cauliflower, squash, mushrooms Greens
- Cabbage, baby bok choy, kale, spinach, or collards Toppings
- Fresh herbs
- Fresh chiles
- Toasted coconut flakes
- Lime wedges
- Green onions: thinly sliced

INSTRUCTIONS:
a) In a huge stockpot, heat the olive oil.
b) Add the garlic and ginger and cook.
c) Stir in the vegetable stock and coconut milk until all is well combined.
d) Then whisk in 3 to 4 tablespoons of curry paste until it has completely dissolved.
e) Taste, and if necessary, add more curry paste.
f) Cover and cook for 5 minutes on low heat. After that, take out the ginger slices.
g) Simmer until ready to serve.
h) Add your preferred dippers, boil and strain them into the bowls using a strainer.
i) Fill each serving bowl with a ladleful of broth.
j) Garnish with preferred toppings and serve hot.

58. Spicy Sweet Potato Kale Cannellini Soup

Makes: 12

INGREDIENTS:
- Parmesan cheese (shredded) 1 cup
- Giardiniera 1/2 cup
- Olive oil as needed
- Heavy whipping cream 1/2 cup
- Fresh kale (chopped) 3 cups
- Cannellini beans (drained and rinsed) 2 cups
- Vegetable broth 1¾ cups
- Pepper 1/4 teaspoon
- Salt 1/2 teaspoon
- Red pepper flakes (crushed) 1 teaspoon
- Sage (rubbed) 1 teaspoon
- Granny smith apples, medium (chopped and peeled) 2
- Sweet potatoes, medium (cubed) 5
- Honey 1 teaspoon
- Garlic cloves (minced) 3
- Onion, medium (finely chopped) 1
- Olive oil 2 tablespoons

INSTRUCTIONS:

a) Take a 6-quart stockpot and heat the oil in it over medium-high flame.

b) Add the onion and cook and mix for 7 to 8 minutes until they become tender.

c) Add the garlic and cook for 1 more minute. Mix into it the broth, seasonings, honey, apples, and sweet potatoes.

d) Boil it ad lower the heat. Simmer it and cover for half an hour until the potatoes become tender.

e) Use an immersion blender to puree the soup or cool the soup slightly and puree it into batches into a blender. Return it into the pan.

f) Add the kale and beans and cook it. Keep it uncovered over medium flame for 15 minutes until the kale turns tender. Stir periodically.

g) Stir the cream into it and serve with the toppings as you desire.

59. Sweet Potato Chicken Stew

Makes: 8

INGREDIENTS:
- Brown rice (hot and cooked) as you like
- Cayenne pepper 1/4 teaspoon
- Dried thyme (divided) 1/2 teaspoon
- Peanut butter (creamy) 1/4 cup
- Chicken broth (reduced-sodium) 1 cup
- Sweet potato, large (peeled and 1-inch cubes cut) 1
- Crushed tomatoes 3 ½ cups
- Black-eyed peas (drained and rinsed) 2 cups
- Fresh ginger root (minced) 2 tablespoons
- Garlic cloves (minced) 6
- Onion, medium (thinly sliced) 1
- Canola oil (divided) 3 teaspoons
- Pepper 1/4 teaspoon
- Salt 1/2 teaspoon
- Chicken breasts (skinless, boneless, and cubed) 2 cups

INSTRUCTIONS:

a) Sprinkle some pepper and salt over the chicken. Cook the chicken over medium flame in two teaspoons of the oil for 5 minutes in a Dutch oven until the chicken is no longer pink; Take the chicken out of the oven and put it aside.

b) Into the same pan, sauté the onion in the oil that is remaining until it becomes tender. Add the ginger and garlic; cook for one more minute.

c) Stir into it the cayenne, 1¼ teaspoons of thyme, peanut butter, broth, sweet potato, tomatoes, and peas.

d) Boil them and lower the heat; cover it and let it simmer for 15 to 20 minutes until the potato becomes tender. Add the chicken and heat through properly.

e) If desired, serve it with rice. Sprinkle using the thyme that is remaining.

60. Sweet Potato Lentil Stew

Makes: 6

INGREDIENTS:
- Fresh cilantro (minced) 1/4 cup
- Vegetable broth 5¼ cups
- Cayenne pepper 1/4 teaspoon
- Ginger, ground 1/4 teaspoon
- Cumin, ground 1/2 teaspoon
- Garlic cloves (minced) 4
- Onion, medium (chopped) 1
- Carrots, medium (cut into pieces 1 inch) 3
- Dried lentils (rinsed) 1½ cups
- Sweet potatoes, medium 2¼ cups

INSTRUCTIONS:
a) Take a 3-quart cooker (slow) and gather the last nine ingredients.
b) Cook them but do not cover.
c) Cook on low flame for 5 to 6 hours until the lentils and vegetables become tender. Mix into it the cilantro.

61. Callaloo Soup

Preparation Time: 20 minutes
Cooking Time: 1 hour
Makes: 4-6 servings

INGREDIENTS
- 6 cups of callaloo or spinach
- 1½ cups of sweet potato diced
- 1½ cups of butternut squash, diced
- 1 onion sliced
- 4 garlic cloves minced
- ½ tablespoon of dried thyme
- ¼ of a scotch bonnet not too much
- 1 teaspoon of Himalayan pink salt
- 1 scallion or 3 ones chopped
- ¼ teaspoon of black pepper
- 4-5 okras sliced
- 2 cups of vegetable stock
- 2 cups of coconut milk
- 2 tablespoons of coconut oil

INSTRUCTIONS

a) Preheat a heavy saucepan over medium heat before adding the coconut oil.

b) Sauté the garlic, onion, and scallion for one minute, or until the onions are tender.

c) Add the diced butternut, sweet potato, and okra.

d) Allow the vegetables to sweat in the pan for two to three minutes, stirring constantly to prevent burning.

e) Add the scotch bonnet, thyme, salt, and pepper while tossing the vegetables.

f) Add the spinach or callaloo to the pan.

g) Add the coconut milk and vegetable stock, then turn the heat to low.

h) Cover the pan with the lid and let the mixture simmer until it thickens, up to an hour.

i) Once the required thickness has been achieved, you can pulse with an immersion stick blender to achieve a more soup-like consistency.

62. Chickpea Sweet Potato Stew

Makes: 4

INGREDIENTS:
- 15oz chickpeas, drained and rinsed
- 2 cups sweet potato, peeled and diced
- 4 tablespoons vegetable broth
- 15oz fire-roasted crushed tomato, 1 can
- 3 cloves garlic, minced
- 1 small onion, diced
- 1 teaspoon ginger, minced
- 3 cups vegetable broth
- 5oz fresh spinach
- 1/4 teaspoon dried coriander
- 1/8 teaspoon cayenne
- 1 tablespoon sweet paprika
- 1/2 teaspoon cumin

INSTRUCTIONS:
a) In a large pot or oven, heat the vegetable broth over medium heat. Once the broth simmers, cook the onion for 4-5 minutes or until it is translucent.
b) Stir in the garlic and ginger for at least 2 to 3 minutes. Cook and stir it occasionally until fragrant, then add sweet paprika, cumin, coriander, and cayenne.
c) Bring the chickpeas, sweet potatoes, crushed tomatoes, and vegetable broth to a boil in a saucepan. Reduce heat to medium-low and let the sweet potatoes cook for 15-20 minutes, or until tender.
d) Stir in the spinach until it is softened. Serve immediately.

63. Coconut Curry Lentils

Makes: 10

INGREDIENTS:
- 2 cups brown lentils
- 14oz can coconut milk, full fat
- 3 tablespoons curry powder
- 2 cloves garlic
- 1 yellow onion
- 15oz tomato sauce
- 1 3/4 lb. sweet potato
- 3 cups vegetable broth
- 2 carrots
- 15oz petite diced tomatoes
- 1/4 teaspoon ground cloves

FOR SERVING
- 1/2 red onion
- 1/2 bunch fresh cilantro
- 10 cups cooked rice

INSTRUCTIONS:

a) Mince the garlic and dice the onion. Slice the peeled carrots and chop the sweet potato into ¼ to ½-inch cubes.

b) In a slow cooker, combine the garlic, onion, sweet potato, carrots, lentils, curry powder, cloves, diced tomatoes, tomato sauce, and vegetable broth. Stir everything together.

c) Set the slow cooker setting to high for 4 hours or low for 7-8 hours. When the lentils are finished, they should be tender and most of the liquid absorbed.

d) Combine the lentils and the coconut milk in a mixing bowl. Adjust the salt or other spices to taste.

e) For serving, place 1 cup cooked rice in a bowl, followed by 1 cup lentil mixture.

f) Serve garnished with finely diced red onion and fresh cilantro.

PASTA

64. Chestnut and Sweet potato Gnocchi

Makes: 4 Servings

INGREDIENTS:
GNOCCHI
- 1 + ½ cup of Roasted sweet potato
- ½ cup Chestnut Flour
- ½ cup Whole milk ricotta
- 2 teaspoons kosher salt
- ½ cup gluten-free flour
- White pepper to taste
- Smoked paprika to taste

MUSHROOM & CHESTNUT RAGU
- 1 cup button mushroom, cut in 4
- 2-3 portobello mushrooms, sliced into fine strips
- 1 tray of shimeji mushrooms (white or brown)
- ⅓ cup of chestnut, diced
- 2 tablespoons of butter
- 2 shallots, finely chopped
- 2 garlic cloves, finely chopped
- 1 teaspoon tomato paste
- White wine (to taste)
- Kosher salt (to taste)
- 2 tablespoons fresh Sage, finely chopped
- Parsley to taste

TO FINISH
- 2 tablespoons of olive oil
- Parmesan Cheese (to taste)

INSTRUCTIONS:

GNOCCHI

a) Preheat the oven to 380 degrees.

b) Pierce the sweet potatoes all over with a fork.

c) Place the sweet potatoes on a rimmed baking sheet and roast for about 30 minutes, or until tender. Let cool slightly.

d) Peel the sweet potatoes and transfer them to a food processor. Puree until smooth.

e) In a large bowl, combine the dry ingredients (chestnut flour, salt, gluten-free flour, white pepper, and smoked paprika), and keep them on the side.

f) Transfer the sweet potato puree to a large bowl. Add in the ricotta and add ¾ of the dried mix. Transfer the dough to a heavily floured work surface and gently knead in more flour until the dough comes together but is still very soft.

g) Divide the dough into 6-8 pieces and roll each piece into a 1-inch-thick rope.

h) Cut the ropes into 1-inch lengths and dust each piece with gluten-free flour.

i) Roll each gnocchi against the tines of a floured fork to make small indentations.

j) Keep it on a tray in the chiller until you are ready to use it.

MUSHROOM & CHESTNUT RAGU

k) In a hot pan, melt the butter and add a pinch of salt.

l) Add the shallots, garlic, and sage and sauté for 10 minutes until the shallots are translucent.

m) Add all the mushrooms and sauté on high heat, stirring constantly.

n) Add the tomato paste and white wine and let it reduce until the mushrooms are soft and tender.

o) Top the ragu with fresh chopped parsley and diced chestnuts. Set aside.

TO FINISH

p) Bring a large pot of salted water to a boil. Add the sweet potato gnocchi and cook until they float to the surface, about 3-4 minutes.

q) Using a slotted spoon, transfer the gnocchi to a large plate. Repeat with the remaining gnocchi.

r) Melt 2 tablespoons of olive oil in a large sauté pan.

s) Add the gnocchi, stirring gently, until the gnocchi is caramelized.

t) Add the mushroom Ragu and add a few tablespoons of the gnocchi water.

u) Stir gently and let it cook for 2-3 minutes on High heat.

v) Serve with a sprinkle of Parmesan cheese on top.

65. Bucatini with Pesto and Sweet Potatoes

Makes: 4 Servings

INGREDIENTS:

- 1 sweet potato, peeled and cut into cubes
- 1 red onion, cut into small wedges
- 1/3 cup + 2 Tablespoons. of olive oil, evenly divided
- Dash of salt and black pepper
- 4 cups of kale, fresh and torn
- ½ cup of parsley, flat leaf and fresh
- 2 ounces of parmesan cheese, freshly grated and extra for serving
- 1 clove of garlic
- 2 teaspoons. of lemon zest
- 1 ½ Tablespoons. of lemon juice, fresh
- 12 ounces of bucatini
- Pine nuts, lightly toasted and for serving

INSTRUCTIONS:

a) First, heat up the oven to 425 degrees.

b) While the oven is heating up, use a large baking sheet and add in the cubed potatoes, onion wedges, and the two tablespoon of olive oil. Toss to mix. Season with a dash of salt and black pepper.

c) Place into the oven to bake for 24 to 26 minutes or until the potatoes and onion wedges are soft.

d) During this time place the kale and chopped parsley into a food processor. Pulse 5 times or until chopped. Then add in the parmesan cheese, garlic clove, fresh lemon zest, and fresh lemon juice. Pulse again for another 12 times.

e) Slowly drizzle the remaining 1/3 cup of olive oil into the mixture and continue to pulse. Season with a dash of salt and black pepper.

f) Next, cook the pasta in boiling water until soft. Once cooked, drain the pasta and set aside. Make sure to reserve ¼ cup of the pasta water.

g) Add the cooked pasta, freshly made pesto, and roasted vegetables into a large bowl. Toss to mix. Pour in the pasta water and toss again to mix.

h) Serve immediately with a topping of parmesan cheese and the toasted pine nuts.

66. Chestnut and Sweet potato Gnocchi

Makes: 4 Servings

INGREDIENTS:
GNOCCHI
- 1 + ½ cup of Roasted sweet potato
- ½ cup Chestnut Flour
- ½ cup Whole milk ricotta
- 2 teaspoons kosher salt
- ½ cup gluten-free flour
- White pepper to taste
- Smoked paprika to taste

MUSHROOM & CHESTNUT RAGU
- 1 cup button mushroom, cut in 4
- 2-3 portobello mushrooms, sliced into fine strips
- 1 tray of shimeji mushrooms (white or brown)
- 1/3 cup of chestnut, diced
- 2 tablespoons of butter
- 2 shallots, finely chopped
- 2 garlic cloves, finely chopped
- 1 teaspoon tomato paste
- White wine (to taste)
- Kosher salt (to taste)
- 2 tablespoons fresh Sage, finely chopped
- Parsley to taste

TO FINISH
- 2 tablespoons of olive oil
- Parmesan Cheese (to taste)

INSTRUCTIONS:

GNOCCHI

a) Preheat the oven to 380 degrees.

b) Pierce the sweet potatoes all over with a fork.

c) Place the sweet potatoes on a rimmed baking sheet and roast for about 30 minutes, or until tender. Let cool slightly.

d) Peel the sweet potatoes and transfer them to a food processor. Puree until smooth.

e) In a large bowl, combine the dry ingredients (chestnut flour, salt, gluten-free flour, white pepper, and smoked paprika), and keep them on the side.

f) Transfer the sweet potato puree to a large bowl. Add in the ricotta and add ¾ of the dried mix. Transfer the dough to a heavily floured work surface and gently knead in more flour until the dough comes together but is still very soft.

g) Divide the dough into 6-8 pieces and roll each piece into a 1-inch-thick rope.

h) Cut the ropes into 1-inch lengths and dust each piece with gluten-free flour.

i) Roll each gnocchi against the tines of a floured fork to make small indentations.

j) Keep it on a tray in the chiller until you are ready to use it.

MUSHROOM & CHESTNUT RAGU

k) In a hot pan, melt the butter and add a pinch of salt.

l) Add the shallots, garlic, and sage and sauté for 10 minutes until the shallots are translucent.

m) Add all the mushrooms and sauté on high heat, stirring constantly.

n) Add the tomato paste and white wine and let it reduce until the mushrooms are soft and tender.

o) Top the ragu with fresh chopped parsley and diced chestnuts. Set aside.

TO FINISH

p) Bring a large pot of salted water to a boil. Add the sweet potato gnocchi and cook until they float to the surface, about 3-4 minutes.

q) Using a slotted spoon, transfer the gnocchi to a large plate. Repeat with the remaining gnocchi.

r) Melt 2 tablespoons of olive oil in a large sauté pan.

s) Add the gnocchi, stirring gently, until the gnocchi is caramelized.

t) Add the mushroom Ragu and add a few tablespoons of the gnocchi water.

u) Stir gently and let it cook for 2-3 minutes on High heat.

v) Serve with a sprinkle of Parmesan cheese on top.

SIDES

67. <u>Lime and tequila sweet potatoes</u>

Makes: 1 servings

INGREDIENTS:
- 2 pounds Sweet potatoes; peeled
- ¼ cup Fresh lime juice
- 2 tablespoons Honey
- 1 tablespoon Tequila

INSTRUCTIONS:

a) Cut sweet potatoes into ¾ inch thick slices. Boil slices in a large pan on high heat for about 6 minutes. Drain. Sweet potatoes should be just tender. In a bowl mix together lime juice, honey and tequila.

b) Brush over potatoes. Grill on greased grate for 4 to 6 minutes. Brush repeatedly with mixture and turn frequently. Sweet potatoes are done when they are browned.

68. Sweet Potato Bacon Mash

Makes: 4

INGREDIENTS:
- 3 sweet potatoes, peeled
- 4 ounces bacon, chopped
- 1 cup chicken stock
- 1 tablespoon butter
- 1 teaspoon salt
- 2 ounces Parmesan, grated

INSTRUCTIONS:
a) Dice sweet potato and put it in the pan.
b) Add chicken stock and close the lid.
c) Boil the vegetables until they are soft.
d) After this, drain the chicken stock.
e) Mash the sweet potato with the help of the potato masher. Add grated cheese and butter.
f) Mix up together salt and chopped bacon. Fry the mixture until it is crunchy (10-15 minutes).
g) Add cooked bacon to the mashed sweet potato and mix up with the help of the spoon.
h) It is recommended to serve the meal warm or hot.

69. Stir-Fried Sweet Potatoes with Parmesan

Makes: 2

INGREDIENTS:
- 2 sweet potatoes, peeled
- ½ yellow onion, sliced
- ½ cup cream
- ¼ cup spinach
- 2 ounces Parmesan cheese, shredded
- ½ teaspoon salt
- 1 tomato
- 1 teaspoon olive oil

INSTRUCTIONS:
a) Chop the sweet potatoes.
b) Chop the tomato.
c) Chop the spinach.
d) Spray the air fryer tray with the olive oil.
e) Then place on the layer of the chopped sweet potato.
f) Add the layer of the sliced onion.
g) After this, sprinkle the sliced onion with the chopped spinach and tomatoes.
h) Sprinkle the casserole with salt and shredded cheese.
i) Pour cream.
j) Preheat the air fryer to 390 F.
k) Cover the air fryer tray with the foil.
l) Cook the casserole for 35 minutes.

70. Sweet Potatoes with Tamarind

Makes: 4

INGREDIENTS:
- 1 tablespoon fresh lemon juice
- 4 sweet potatoes, peeled and cubed
- ¼ teaspoon black salt
- 1½ tablespoons Tamarind Chutney
- ½ teaspoon cumin seeds, roasted and roughly pounded

INSTRUCTIONS:
a) Cook sweet potatoes for 7 minutes in salted water, until fork-tender.
b) Drain and set aside to cool.
c) Combine all of the ingredients in a mixing bowl and gently toss.
d) Serve in bowls with toothpicks inserted into the cubed sweet potatoes.

71. Fall vegetables on the grill

Makes: 1 serving

Ingredients
- 2 potatoes, diced
- 1 Acorn squash, diced
- ¼ cup Butter; melted
- 1 tablespoon thyme
- Salt and pepper to taste
- 2 Sweet potatoes, diced
- 3 tablespoons Vegetable oil

Directions
a) Prepare the grill for indirect grilling.
b) Combine vegetables, oil, salt, and pepper in a mixing bowl.
c) On a small plate, combine the butter and the thyme.
d) Place vegetables on the grill.
e) Cook for 15 minutes with the top closed.
f) Turn, brush with the butter and thyme mixture and cook for another 15 minutes until the vegetables are soft.

72. Chimichurri grilled vegetables

Makes 4 Servings

Ingredients
- 1/2 cup olive oil
- 2 teaspoons fresh thyme
- 2 shallots, quartered
- 3 garlic cloves, crushed
- 1/3 cup fresh parsley leaves
- 1/4 cup fresh basil leaves
- 1/2 teaspoon salt
- 2 tablespoons fresh lemon juice
- 1 red onion, quartered
- 1 sweet potato, peeled and diced
- 1 zucchini, cut diagonally
- 2 ripe plantains, halved lengthwise
- 1/4 teaspoon black pepper

Directions
a) Preheat the grill.
b) In a food processor, finely mince the shallots and garlic.
c) Pulse until the parsley, basil, thyme, salt, and pepper are finely minced. Process until the lemon juice and olive oil are well combined. Move to a small bowl.
d) Brush the vegetables with the Chimichurri sauce.
e) Put them on the grill to cook.
f) Continue to grill until the vegetables are soft, 10 to 15 minutes for everything except the plantains, which should be done in 7 minutes.
g) Serve immediately with a dash of the leftover sauce.

73. Roasted-Garlic Sweet Potatoes

4 servings

Ingredients
- 1-1/2 pounds unpeeled sweet potatoes, cut into 1/2-inch pieces
- 12 cloves garlic, peeled and cut in half
- 1 tablespoon extra-virgin olive oil
- 1–2 tablespoons minced Serrano or jalapeño chile 3/4 teaspoon dried thyme 1/2 teaspoon kosher salt
- 1/2 teaspoon pepper

Directions
a) Preheat your oven and pan. Place a 12-inch ovenproof skillet or casserole dish large enough to hold the potatoes in a single layer in the oven, turn the heat to 375°F, and heat the pan for 30 minutes.

b) Mix the ingredients. While the skillet is heating, combine all the ingredients in a bowl.

c) Roast the potatoes. Remove the heated skillet from the oven and immediately evenly distribute the mixed Ingredients. Put the skillet in the oven and roast the potatoes for 45 minutes, stirring every 15 minutes so they will cook evenly.

74. Sous Vide Maple Glazed Sweet Potatoes

Servings: 6

INGREDIENTS:
- 2-1/2 pounds sweet potatoes, peeled and cut into 1-1/2-inch pieces
- 1/3 cup pure maple syrup
- 2 tablespoons butter, melted
- 1 tablespoon lemon juice
- 1/2 teaspoon salt

INSTRUCTIONS:
a) Set your Anova to 190F/87.7C.
b) Combine all the ingredients in a vacuum-sealed bag.
c) Submerge the bag in the water bath and cook for at least 60 minutes and not longer than 90 minutes.
d) Remove from bag and drizzle the liquid over the potatoes to serve.

75. Bacon & Sweet Potatoes

SERVINGS: 4

INGREDIENTS:
- ½ cup orange juice
- 4 bacon slices, cooked and crumbled
- 4 pounds sweet potatoes, sliced
- 3 tablespoons agave nectar
- ½ teaspoon thyme, dried
- ½ teaspoon sage, crushed
- 1 teaspoon curry powder
- A pinch of sea salt and black pepper
- 2 tablespoons olive oil

INSTRUCTIONS:

a) In your instant pot, combine sweet potato slices, orange juice, agave nectar, thyme, sage, curry, sea salt, black pepper, olive oil, and bacon.

b) Cook on High for 10 minutes, covered.

c) Transfer to breakfast plates and serve.

76. Gouda Mixed Potato Mash

Makes: 12

INGREDIENTS:
- Pepper 1/2 teaspoon
- Paprika 1 teaspoon
- Salt 1/2 teaspoon
- Gouda cheese (shredded) 1 cup
- 2% milk 1/2 cup
- Sweet potatoes, medium (cubed and peeled) 2 Yukon gold potatoes, medium (cubed and peeled) 6

INSTRUCTIONS:
a) Place sweet potatoes and Yukon Gold into a Dutch oven. Add water to cover the ingredients. Boil them, and then lower the heat.
b) Cook it, but leave it uncovered for 10 to 15 minutes until they become tender. Drain them and put them back into the pan.
c) Mash the potatoes and gradually add the milk. Mix into it the pepper, salt, paprika, and cheese.

77. **Two-Tone Baked Sweet Potatoes**

Makes: 12

INGREDIENTS:
- Salt (divided) 1½ teaspoons
- Fresh chives (minced and divided) 4 tablespoons Cheddar cheese (shredded) ¾ cup 2% milk 1/3 cup
- Sour cream (divided) 2/3 cup
- Sweet potatoes, medium 6
- Russet potatoes, medium 6

INSTRUCTIONS:
a) To 400 degrees F, preheat the oven. Scrub the sweet potatoes and the russet; use a fork to Pierce them several times. Place it into foil-lined pans (15×10×1).
b) Bake for 1 hour to 1 hour 10 minutes until they become tender. Reduce the settings of the oven to 350 degrees F.
c) When it is cool enough to hold the handle, cut all the russet potatoes one-third from the top. Discard all the tops and save the others.
d) Scoop out the pulp and leave only ½ inches thick shells. Take a bowl, mash the pulp, add 1/3 cup of sour cream, ¾ teaspoon of salt, 2 tablespoons of choices, cheese, and milk.
e) Spoon the mixture of russet potato into half of every sweet potato skin and russet.
f) Spoon the mixture of sweet potato into another half. Return it to the pan.
g) Bake for 15 to 20 minutes until it is properly heated.

78. Chili sweet potato gratin

Makes: 6 Servings

INGREDIENTS:
- 2 cans (10-ounce) mild enchilada sauce (2 cups)
- 1 cup Water
- 2 larges Garlic
- Cloves; minced and mashed to a paste
- 5 larges Sweet potatoes; (about 3 1/2 lbs)
- 1⅓ cup Coarsely grated Monterey Jack cheese; (about 6 ounces)

INSTRUCTIONS:

a) Preheat oven to 375F. In a large saucepan simmer enchilada sauce, water, and garlic with salt to taste, stirring occasionally, 5 minutes.

b) Peel potatoes and cut crosswise into ⅛-inch-thick slices. In a 3-quart gratin or shallow baking dish layer one fourth of potatoes in concentric circles, overlapping slightly, and sprinkle with ⅓ cup cheese. Continue to layer remaining potatoes and cheese in same manner, ending with cheese.

c) Pour sauce slowly over potatoes, letting it seep between layers, and bake gratin set in a shallow baking pan (it may bubble over) in middle of oven 1 hour, or until potatoes are tender.

d) Gratin may be made 2 days ahead and chilled, covered.

e) Reheat gratin, covered, in oven.

SALADS

79. Arugula and Sweet Potato Salad

Makes: 4

INGREDIENTS:
- 1 pound sweet potatoes
- 1 cup walnuts
- 1 tablespoon olive oil
- 1 cup water
- 1 tablespoon soy sauce
- 3 cups arugula

INSTRUCTIONS:
a) Bake potatoes at 400 F until tender, remove and set aside
b) In a bowl drizzle, walnuts with olive oil and microwave for 2-3 minutes or until toasted
c) In a bowl combine all salad ingredients and mix well
d) Pour over soy sauce and serve

80. Autumn Harvest Salad

Makes 4 servings

INGREDIENTS:
- 1 pound sweet potatoes, peeled and cut into 1/2-inch dice
- 1 tablespoon pure maple syrup
- 1/2 teaspoon Dijon mustard
- 1/2 teaspoon salt
- 2 tablespoons apple cider vinegar
- 1/3 cup grapeseed oil
- 1 ripe Bosc pear
- 1 crisp red-skinned apple, such as Red Delicious, Fuji, or Gala
- 2 celery ribs, chopped
- 1/2 cup toasted walnuts or pecans
- 1/4 cup sweetened dried cranberries
- 2 green onions, minced

INSTRUCTIONS:
a) In a large saucepan of boiling salted water, cook the sweet potatoes until just tender, about 20 minutes. Drain well, place in a large bowl, and set aside.
b) In a separate large bowl, combine the maple syrup, mustard, salt, and vinegar. Whisk in the oil until well blended. Set aside.
c) Core the pear and apple and cut into 1/2-inch dice. Add them to the bowl with the dressing, and
d) toss to coat. Add the pear and apple mixture to the sweet potatoes. Add the celery, walnuts, cranberries, and green onions. Toss gently to combine and serve.

81. Sweet Potato And Broccoli With Pomegranate Dressing

Makes 4 to 6 servings

INGREDIENTS:
- 3 sweet potatoes, unpeeled
- 2 cups lightly steamed broccoli florets
- 3 celery ribs, cut into 1/4-inch slices
- 4 green onions, minced
- 2 tablespoons chopped fresh parsley
- 1/4 cup creamy peanut butter
- 1 teaspoon minced fresh ginger
- 1/4 cup grapeseed oil
- 1/4 cup fresh lemon juice
- 1/2 teaspoon sugar
- Salt and freshly ground black pepper
- 1/4 cup crushed unsalted roasted peanuts, for garnish
- 2 tablespoons fresh pomegranate seeds or 1/4 cup sweetened dried cranberries, for garnish

INSTRUCTIONS:
a) In a large saucepan, bring the sweet potatoes and enough water to cover to boil over high heat.
b) Reduce heat to medium and simmer until tender, but still firm, about 30 minutes. Drain and cool, then peel them and cut into 1/2-inch chunks and transfer to a large bowl. Add the broccoli, celery, green onions, and parsley. Set aside.
c) In a small bowl, combine the peanut butter, ginger, oil, lemon juice, sugar, and salt and pepper to taste. Pour the dressing over the salad and toss gently to combine.
d) Garnish with peanuts and pomegranate seeds and serve.

82. Collard Green Salad with Sweet Potatoes

Makes: serves 6-8

Ingredients

- 2 lb. sweet potatoes, peeled and cut crosswise into 1/2-inch-thick slices
- 1/4 cup plus 2 tbsp. red palm oil or vegetable oil
- 1 tbsp. cumin seeds
- 1 tbsp. thyme leaves
- 2 cloves garlic
- Kosher salt and freshly ground black pepper
- 2 tbsp. fresh lime juice
- 1 tsp. minced ginger
- 1 lb. collard greens, stems removed, leaves thinly shredded (6 cups)
- 2 oz. goat cheese, crumbled
- 1/4 cup roasted, unsalted cashews, roughly chopped

Directions

a) Heat the oven to 400°. On a rimmed baking sheet, toss the sweet potato slices with 2 tablespoons of the palm oil, the cumin, thyme, and garlic. Season with salt and pepper and roast the sweet potatoes, flipping once halfway through cooking, until golden brown, about 40 minutes. Transfer the potatoes to a rack and let cool.

b) Meanwhile, in a small bowl, combine the lime juice and ginger and let stand for 10 minutes to soften. Whisk in the remaining 1/4 cup palm oil until emulsified and then season the vinaigrette with salt and pepper.

c) To serve, place the collard greens in a large bowl and toss with 1 tablespoon of the dressing, massaging it into the greens for about 5 minutes. Transfer the greens to a serving platter, top with the sweet potatoes, and sprinkle with the goat cheese and cashews.

d) Serve with the remaining dressing on the side.

83. Sweet Potato Salad with almonds

Makes: 6

INGREDIENTS:
- 3 pounds sweet potatoes, peeled and cut into ¾-inch pieces
- 6 tablespoons extra-virgin olive oil, divided
- 2 teaspoons table salt
- 3 scallions, sliced thin
- 3 tablespoons lime juice (2 limes)
- 1 jalapeño chile, stemmed, seeded, and minced
- 1 teaspoon ground cumin
- 1 teaspoon smoked paprika
- 1 teaspoon pepper
- 1 garlic clove, minced
- ½ teaspoon ground allspice
- ½ cup fresh cilantro leaves and stems, chopped coarse
- ½ cup whole almonds, toasted and chopped

INSTRUCTIONS:

a) Adjust oven rack to middle position and heat oven to 450 degrees. Toss potatoes with 2 tablespoons oil and salt, then transfer to rimmed baking sheet and spread into even layer. Roast until potatoes are tender and just beginning to brown, 30 to 40 minutes, stirring halfway through roasting. Let potatoes cool for 30 minutes.

b) Meanwhile, combine scallions, lime juice, jalapeño, cumin, paprika, pepper, garlic, allspice, and remaining ¼ cup oil in large bowl. Add cilantro, almonds, and potatoes and toss to combine. Serve.

84. Quinoa Mango Salad With Mashed Potatoes

Makes: 3

INGREDIENTS:
1. 1 cup quinoa (millet)
2. 1 cup radishes
3. 2 tablespoons olive oil
4. 2 teaspoons salt
5. 1 teaspoon black pepper
6. Some kale leaves
7. ½ cup cashew nuts
8. 5 mangoes, sliced
9. 2 Sweet potatoes, diced
10. 1 tablespoon lemon juice
11. 3 cloves garlic, crushed
12. ¼ avocado diced

INSTRUCTIONS:
a) Set your instant pot to the stir-fry setting
b) Pour in the olive oil and garlic
c) Stir for about 2 minutes
d) Add the quinoa and keep stirring for 5 minutes
e) Add the kale and radishes, and stir fry for another 3 minutes
f) Remove this from the instant pot and place them in serving plates
g) Place water into the instant pot
h) Add the potatoes, salt, lemon juice and black pepper
i) Cover your instant pot and boil potatoes for 5 minutes
j) Smash the potatoes and add the avocado and mangoes
k) Serve with the stir fried kale
l) Be sure to be creative with your serving method

85. Grilled Three-Potato Salad

Makes: 6

INGREDIENTS:
- Pepper 1/4 teaspoon
- Celery seed 1/2 teaspoon
- Salt 1 teaspoon
- Dijon mustard 1 tablespoon
- White wine vinegar 3 tablespoons
- Canola oil 1/4 cup
- Green onions (thinly sliced) 1/ cup
- Sweet potato, medium (peeled) 1
- Red potatoes 1 ¾ cup
- Yukon gold potatoes 1 ¾ cup

INSTRUCTIONS:
a) Place the sweet potato and the potatoes in a Dutch oven; cover it and let it simmer for 15 to 20 minutes until they turn tender.
b) Drain the mixture and cool it down. Cut it into chunks of 1 inch each.
c) Put the mixture of potatoes in a basket or a grill wok. Grill it for 10 to 12 minutes over medium flame until it turns brown. Stir periodically.
d) Transfer the mixture into a large-sized salad bowl; add the onions.
e) Whisk the pepper, celery seed, salt, mustard, vinegar, and oil.
f) Drizzle over the mixture of potato and toss well to coat properly.
g) Serve it at room temperature or just warm.

86. Roasted Sweet Potato and Prosciutto Salad

Makes: 8

INGREDIENTS:
- Honey 1 teaspoon
- Lemon juice 1 tablespoon
- Green onions (divided and sliced) 2
- Sweet red pepper (finely chopped) 1/4 cup
- Pecans (chopped and toasted) 1/3 cup
- Radishes (sliced) 1/2 cup
- Prosciutto (thinly sliced and julienned) 1/2 cup
- Pepper 1/8 teaspoon
- 1/2 teaspoonSalt (divided)
- 4 tablespoons Olive oil (divided)
- 3 Sweet potatoes, medium (peeled and cubed into 1-inch)

INSTRUCTIONS:
a) To 400 degrees F, preheat the oven. Place the sweet potatoes in a greased baking pan (15x10x1 inches).

b) Drizzle 2 tablespoons of oil and sprinkle 1/4 teaspoon of salt and pepper and toss them properly. Roast for half an hour, and still periodically.

c) Sprinkle some prosciutto over the sweet potatoes and roast it for 10 to 15 minutes until the sweet potatoes are tender and the prosciutto is turned crispy.

d) Transfer the mixture to a large-sized bowl, and let it cool down slightly.

e) Add half of the green onions, red pepper, pecans, and radishes. Take a small-sized bowl, whisk the salt, the remaining oil, honey, and lemon juice until well blended.

f) Drizzle it over the salad; toss properly to combine. Sprinkle with the remaining green onions.

87. Roasted Vegetable and Polenta Salad

Makes: 4 servings

Ingredients
- 2 medium sweet potatoes, cut into 3/4-inch pieces
- 1 small head broccoli, florets and stems chopped
- 1 small red onion, cut into 3/4-inch wedges
- 1 cup cherry or grape tomatoes
- 5 tablespoons extra-virgin olive oil
- Kosher salt and freshly ground pepper
- 2 tablespoons white wine vinegar
- 1 18-ounce tube prepared polenta
- 12 large sage leaves
- 1 5-ounce package mixed baby salad greens
- 2 ounces goat cheese

INSTRUCTIONS:

a) Place a rimmed baking sheet in the middle of the oven and preheat to 450° F. Combine the sweet potatoes, broccoli, red onion and tomatoes in a bowl. Add 2 tablespoons olive oil, 3/4 teaspoon salt and a generous amount of pepper; toss well. Spread out on the hot pan and roast, stirring once or twice, until the vegetables are browned, 25 to 30 minutes. Drizzle with 1 tablespoon vinegar, scraping up any stuck bits from the bottom of the pan.

b) Meanwhile, cut the polenta into 1 1/2-inch pieces (about 24). Heat 2 more tablespoons olive oil in a large nonstick skillet over medium-high heat. Add the sage leaves and cook until crisp, 1 to 2 minutes. Transfer to a paper towel to drain. Add the polenta pieces to the remaining oil in the skillet; season with salt and pepper. Cook, turning occasionally, until the polenta pieces release easily from the pan and are golden and crisp, 15 to 20 minutes.

c) Toss the salad greens with the remaining 1 tablespoon each olive oil and vinegar and a pinch each of salt and pepper. Divide among shallow bowls. Top evenly with the warm roasted vegetables and polenta along with any extra olive oil from the skillet. Break the goat cheese into bits and sprinkle over the salad. Tear the fried sage and sprinkle on top.

88. Roasted Sweet Potatoes & Fresh Figs

SERVES 4

INGREDIENTS
- 4 small sweet potatoes (2¼ lb / 1 kg in total)
- 5 tbsp olive oil
- 3 tbsp / 40 ml balsamic vinegar (you can use a commercial rather than a premium aged grade)
- 1½ tbsp / 20 g superfine sugar
- 12 green onions, halved lengthwise and cut into 1½-in / 4cm segments
- 1 red chile, thinly sliced
- 6 ripe figs (8½ oz / 240 g in total), quartered
- 5 oz / 150 g soft goat's milk cheese (optional)
- Maldon sea salt and freshly ground black pepper

INSTRUCTIONS
a) Preheat the oven to 475°F / 240°C.

b) Wash the sweet potatoes, halve them lengthwise, and then cut each half again similarly into 3 long wedges. Mix with 3 tablespoons of the olive oil, 2 teaspoons salt, and some black pepper. Spread the wedges out, skin side down, on a baking sheet and cook for about 25 minutes, until soft but not mushy. Remove from the oven and leave to cool down.

c) To make the balsamic reduction, place the balsamic vinegar and sugar in a small saucepan. Bring to a boil, then decrease the heat and simmer for 2 to 4 minutes, until it thickens. Be sure to remove the pan from the heat when the vinegar is still runnier than honey; it will continue to thicken as it cools. Stir in a drop of water before serving if it does become too thick to drizzle.

d) Arrange the sweet potatoes on a serving platter. Heat the remaining oil in a medium saucepan over medium heat and add the green onions and chile. Fry for 4 to 5 minutes, stirring often to make sure not to burn the chile. Spoon the oil, onions, and chile over the sweet potatoes. Dot the figs among the wedges and then drizzle over the balsamic reduction. Serve at room temperature. Crumble the cheese over the top, if using.

89. Caesar Salad with BBQ Sweet Potato Croutons

Makes: 2

INGREDIENTS:
SALAD
- 1 batch BBQ roasted sweet potato croutons
- 1 cup carrots, shredded
- 2 heads romaine lettuce hearts, rinsed, dried, roughly chopped
- 2 tablespoons nutritional yeast
- 1 cup roughly chopped parsley

DRESSING
- 1/2 cup plain hummus
- 4 cloves garlic, minced
- 1 1/2 teaspoon spicy mustard
- 2 tablespoons lemon juice
- 2 teaspoons maple syrup
- 1 teaspoon vegetable broth
- 2 teaspoons capers, chopped
- 2 teaspoons caper brining juice
- 1/2 teaspoon lemon zest

1 healthy pinch sea salt

INSTRUCTIONS:

a) Prepare the dressing in a mixing bowl. Simply combine the hummus, garlic, spicy mustard, lemon zest and juice, capers, maple syrup, brining juice, salt, and pepper.

b) Toss to combine and add a little water to thin the consistency and make it easier to pour. Whisk the mixture until it is creamy and smooth.

c) Season with salt and pepper, lemon zest for vibrant citrus flavor, juice for acidity, garlic for the zing flavor, capers for the sea-like taste, mustard for spice, maple syrup for sweetness, and vegetable broth.

d) Prepare the remaining ingredients, which should include Romaine lettuce, parsley, and shredded carrots. Then, transfer everything to a serving bowl and top with sweet potatoes and nutritional yeast, if desired.

e) Mix in the dressing to coat everything in flavor. Serve and enjoy!

90. Sweet Potato & Avocado Green Salad

Makes: 1

INGREDIENTS:
- Sweet Potato
- 1 large organic sweet potato
- 1 tablespoon vegetable broth
- 1 pinch sea salt
- Dressing
- 1/4 cup tahini
- 1 tablespoon maple syrup
- 2 tablespoons lemon juice
- 1 pinch sea salt
- Water, to thin
- Salad
- 1 medium ripe avocado, cubed
- 5 cups greens of choice
- 2 tablespoons hemp seeds

INSTRUCTIONS:
a) Preheat your oven to 375 °F. Prepare a baking sheet with parchment paper.
b) Add sweet potatoes, then toss with a bit of vegetable broth and salt. Spread the potatoes into an even layer.
c) Bake for 15 minutes, flipping through to ensure even baking. Bake for another 5-10 minutes, or until the potatoes are tender and golden brown.
d) Using a mixing bowl, combine the tahini, maple syrup, lemon juice, and salt. Whisk to combine, then add a little bit of water at a time until you have a semi-thick consistency.
e) Taste and adjust the flavor depending on your preference. Set aside.
f) Assemble the salad in a serving bowl by layering greens and topping with avocado and roasted sweet potato.
g) Serve with dressing and sprinkle with hemp seeds as an option.

DESSERT

91. Chicken Pie with Sweet Potatoes

Makes: 5 Servings

INGREDIENTS:
- 1 whole chicken puck
- 3 large sweet potatoes
- 2 onions
- 4 cloves garlic
- ½ cup tomato sauce
- 1 cup cooked green banana puree
- 1 tablespoon lard
- 1 cup milk
- Salt, black pepper, and cayenne, paprika, nutmeg, cumin, curry

INSTRUCTIONS:
a) First, cook the chicken breast in water. Prepare it in the pressure cooker and leave 20 minutes since the pot boils.
b) Cook the chicken, prepares the sweet potatoes in water to make the puree.
c) Make the mash stepping potatoes with the butter and go putting the milk to give the consistency that you like. Season with salt, black pepper, and nutmeg.
d) Now that the chicken cooled, you can crush everything tiny.
e) In a saucepan brown the onion with a minimum of oil. Add the garlic, the tomato sauce, and the chicken. Mix well, if this medium dry adds a little water. Go putting the condiments: salt, black pepper, and cayenne, cumin, curry. Try to see if it is to your liking.
f) If you already like how it was great. But if you want a creamier consistency, the green banana puree is ideal, if not an option is to use the milk with the cornstarch.
g) To assemble the dish, put down the sautéed chicken and top with the mashed potatoes. Take to oven under 180 ° C for 20 minutes.

92. Coconut sweet potato pudding

CUISINE:KENYAN

Ingredients (serves 6)
- 1 cup fresh ground coconut
- ½ cups sweet potatoes , boiled or mashed
- eggs
- ¾ cup sugar
- ¾ cup milk
- ½ cup water
- 4 tbsp melted butter
- ½ tsp mixed spices
- ½ tsp cinnamon

INSTRUCTIONS:
a) Mix sugar, sweet potatoes and coconut together with spoon until smooth. Add butter, milk, water and beat thoroughly. Beat the eggs slightly, and then beat the mixture in gradually.

b) Add spices and cinnamon. Continue beating until creamy and very smooth. Pour mixture into a greased dish and bake for 30 minutes in hot oven, until golden brown. You can serve it hot or cold.

93. Sweet Potato Pie Trifle

Makes: 16 servings

INGREDIENTS:
- 1 pecan pie
- 1 sweet potato pie or pumpkin pie
- 2 ½ cups whipped cream
- 2 cups butter pecan ice cream
- 1 cup caramel sauce

INSTRUCTIONS:
a) On the bottom, I start with sweet potato pie and crust which will help it stay sturdy.
b) Next layer with some ice cream then whipped cream. You can add some caramel on top of the whipped cream if you wish.
c) Next, I layer with the pecan pie pieces.
d) Then repeat with ice cream, and whipped cream, and top with caramel and pecans.

94. Sweet Potato Pie Tiramisu

Makes: 16 servings

INGREDIENTS
- 8 ounces mascarpone cheese, softened
- ½ cup granulated sugar plus one tablespoon separated
- ⅓ cup brown sugar packed
- 15 ounces of sweet potato in syrup, drained and mashed
- ½ teaspoon ground cinnamon plus more for garnish
- ¼ teaspoon ground nutmeg
- 2 tablespoons pure vanilla extract separated
- 2 ½ cups fresh whipped cream separated
- ¼ cup warm coffee
- 17.5 ounces ladyfingers
- 6 gingersnaps crumbled

INSTRUCTIONS

TO MAKE FILLING:

a) Add mascarpone cheese and ½ cup of granulated sugar and all brown sugar to a stand mixer and beat until smooth.

b) Next add in mashed sweet potato, cinnamon, nutmeg, and 1 tablespoon of the vanilla extract and beat until well incorporated.

c) Lastly, fold 1 ½ cups whipped cream into the sweet potato mixture and set aside.

TO ASSEMBLE THE TIRAMISU:

d) Add the remaining teaspoon of vanilla extract to a bowl with coffee and stir together.

e) Arrange a full row of ladyfingers at the bottom of a 9-inch springform pan.

f) Pour ½ of the warm coffee mixture over the ladyfingers to soak them.

g) Next, take half of the sweet potato mixture and smooth over the top of the ladyfingers.

h) Next create another layer by repeating all steps starting with adding another row of ladyfingers, pouring coffee sauce on the ladyfingers, and finally adding the rest of the sweet potato mixture.

i) Lastly, take the remaining 1 cup of whipped cream and whisk in the remaining tablespoon of granulated sugar, and spread over the top of the tiramisu.

j) Garnish the top of the tiramisu with crumbled gingersnaps over whipped topping and a little ground cinnamon.

k) Place the springform pan in the refrigerator for at least 4 hours before serving.

95. Cherry-sweet potato bread

Makes: 1 Servings

INGREDIENTS:
- 1¾ cup Flour
- 1 teaspoon Baking soda
- 1 teaspoon Cinnamon
- 3 Eggs
- ½ cup Milk
- ½ cup March; cherries
- 1 can (15 ounce) sweet potato; (or yams) drained
- ¼ cup Chopped pecans or walnuts
- 1½ cup Sugar
- ¼ teaspoon Salt
- 1 teaspoon Pumpkin spice
- ¾ cup Vegetable oil
- ¼ cup Raisins
- 1 teaspoon Vanilla

INSTRUCTIONS:
a) Combine and mix flour, sugar, salt, soda, cinnamon, pumpkin spice well. Add eggs, oil and milk stirring until smooth.
b) Blend in sweet potatoes, raisins, nuts, cherries and vanilla.
c) Pour into well greased bread pan that has been lightly floured. Bake approximately 1 hour at 325 degrees (check at 50 minutes), checking by inserting tester to be sure it is done. Tester will come out clean.

96. Cranberry sweet potato muffins

Makes: 12 Servings

INGREDIENTS:
- 1½ cup Flour
- ½ cup Sugar
- 2 teaspoons Baking powder
- ¾ teaspoon Salt
- ½ teaspoon Cinnamon
- ½ teaspoon Nutmeg
- 1 large Egg
- ½ cup Milk
- ½ cup Sweet potatoes; mashed
- ¼ cup Margarine; melted
- 1 cup Cranberries

INSTRUCTIONS:

a) Combine dry ingredients. Stir combined wet ingredients into dry & stir just until moistened. Fold in cranberries.

b) Fill 12 paper-lined muffin cups about ⅔ full. Sprinkle with cinnamon sugar, if desired.

c) Bake at 375F for 18-22 minutes. Remove from pan to cool.

97. Grated sweet potato pudding

Makes: 1 Serving

INGREDIENTS:
- 4 cups Grated sweet potatoes
- 1 cup Cane syrup
- ½ cup Sugar
- 1 cup Milk
- ½ cup Butter
- 3 Eggs
- ½ cup Chopped nuts
- 1 cup Raisins
- 1 teaspoon Cinnamon
- 1 teaspoon Allspice
- ½ teaspoon Cloves

INSTRUCTIONS:
a) Melt butter in a heavy, oven-proof skillet. Mix all ingredients together.
b) Pour mixture into the hot pan of butter, stir until heated.
c) Put skillet in 350 degrees oven and bake.
d) When crusted around edge and top, turn under and let the crust form again. Do this twice, allowing the last to remain on sides and top, about 40 minutes.
e) Serve with sweetened cream or ice cream.

DRINKS

98. Apple Pie Juice

Makes: 2 Servings

INGREDIENTS:
- 1 sweet potato
- ¼ teaspoon pumpkin pie spice
- 2 apples
- 2 carrots
- 2 oranges

INSTRUCTIONS:
a) Core the apples. Take the rind off sweet potato and oranges. Trim the carrots.
b) Put them into your juice extractor together with pumpkin pie spices.
c) Juice all the ingredients and pour your juice into a couple of glasses.

99. Sweet Potato Pie Protein Shake

Ingredients
- 2 scoops vanilla protein powder
- 6 oz. almond milk
- ½ cup sweet potato (already baked, no skin)
- 1-5 drops vanilla extract
- 4 oz. water (more for a thinner shake, less for a thicker shake)
- Crushed ice
- Pumpkin Pie Spice to taste

Directions
a) Throw all ingredients into a blender for 30-60 seconds.

100. Sweet Potato Shake

Ingredients
- 1 sweet potato, cooked and peeled
- ½ teaspoon cinnamon
- 1/2 cup shredded almonds
- 2 scoops whey protein (any flavor)
- 16 oz. whole milk

Directions
a) Throw all ingredients into a blender for 30-60 seconds.

CONCLUSION

Try these sweet potato recipes and win the hearts of all of your family members. It is assured that they all will praise your cooking skills as you will serve them such delicious and luscious food. You can follow this simple cookbook if you are only trying the recipe or even if you are learning a specific recipe. Serve these dishes at a gathering or just at your home; it will always be worth it, and you will never regret making any of these recipes.

By following the steps as directed, we hope you will find the answers to your question as we tried our best to assist you through all the ways we could. We look forward to you making these recipes for your folks and friends. If you are a beginner or a pro, this cookbook will always be at your help, and the directions of each recipe will make it easy for you to follow.

Here is to hoping that you have a happy and healthy life.

Ingram Content Group UK Ltd.
Milton Keynes UK
UKHW020624210623
423802UK00010B/95